Autonomy or Dependence as Regional Integration Outcomes: Central America

PHILIPPE C. SCHMITTER

RESEARCH SERIES, NO. 17

Institute of International Studies

University of California, Berkeley

INSTITUTE OF INTERNATIONAL STUDIES
UNIVERSITY OF CALIFORNIA, BERKELEY

ERNST B. HAAS,
Director
NEIL J. SMELSER,
Associate Director

The Institute of International Studies was established in 1955 to foster comparative and international research in the social sciences and related fields. It is primarily concerned with contemporary problems, the analysis of which contributes to the development of systematic social science theory. The programs of the Institute are carried on in conjunction with various centers and committees dealing with African, Chinese, Japanese and Korean, Latin American, Middle Eastern, South and Southeast Asian, and Slavic and East European Studies, as well as through projects concerned with problems which cut across geographic areas. Some of the current projects are: International Population and Urban Research, the Politics of Modernization, and the Comparative Study of Communist Societies. In addition to its direct sponsorship of various studies, the Institute is the primary agency on the Berkeley campus for facilitating and coordinating comparative international research programs.

Other Institute monographs, listed on the inside back cover, may be ordered from the Publications Office, Institute of International Studies, University of California, Berkeley, California 94720.

AUTONOMY OR DEPENDENCE AS REGIONAL
INTEGRATION OUTCOMES: CENTRAL AMERICA

Autonomy or Dependence as Regional Integration Outcomes: Central America

PHILIPPE C. SCHMITTER

Institute of International Studies
University of California, Berkeley

Standard Book Number 87725-117-7
Library of Congress Card Number 72-619594
© 1972 by the Regents of the University of California

ACKNOWLEDGMENTS

Field research for this study as well as "time-off" support for an initial contemplation of the conceptual and theoretical issues it raised were generously provided by the Studies in International Integration Project of the Institute of International Studies, University of California, Berkeley. Thanks to the thorough and pitiless criticism of its Director, Ernst B. Haas, and the more diplomatic but equally helpful comments of Stuart Fagan and Joseph S. Nye, Jr. on earlier drafts, I have avoided some inaccuracies of fact and evaluative distortions. I am exclusively responsible for those which remain. I would also like to thank Ilse Luraschi for having struggled through my illegible script and the Committee on Latin American Studies at the University of Chicago for having provided their services.

This monograph is an extension of some interpretative themes and factual information contained in an earlier article: "Central American Integration: Spill-Over, Spill-Around or Encapsulation?," Journal of Common Market Studies, IX (September 1970).

CONTENTS

LIST OF TABLES

Chapter 1

REGIONAL INTEGRATION IN CENTRAL AMERICA:
TOWARD AUTONOMY OR DEPENDENCE?

The analyst of Central American integration is immediately
confronted with a major paradox. He is faced with examining a
process which appears to have no overt opponents, yet which seems
to be locked into a hopeless political stalemate. In principle,
virtually no one opposes the restoration of the area's long lost
unity; in practice, efforts expended in the name of such regional
integration have so far met insurmountable obstacles.

To this disparity between consent in principle and dissent
in practice, perhaps no issue has contributed more than that of
"external penetration"--attempts by extra-regional powers to take
advantage of the newly created regional opportunities and the
consequent fear that these outside powers would derive more benefit from integration than would the intra-regional participants.
On the other hand, no prospect has generated more diffuse public
support for integration than the hope that the new institutions
of regional collaboration would be used actively, even aggressive-
ly, to redress the existing assymetry in power, status, and wealth
between this peripheral area and the dynamic, hegemonic centers
of the world. This latter process, whereby integrating units
jointly elaborate a common position in negotiations with outsiders, is referred to herein as "policy externalization."

Theories--or better, ideologies--in support of regional
integration were initially elaborated in the context of advanced
industrial societies, and were somewhat studiously indifferent
to the externalization issue. Implicitly, if not explicitly,
they accepted the notion of discriminatory impact and assumed
that greater positive benefits would accrue to "insiders" than
to "outsiders." Hence they were denounced by orthodox liberal
economists for their "trade diversion effects" and by universalistic political ideologues for their interference with rational,
global "functionalism."

Integration theorists/promoters in the setting of less
developed, industrializing societies were more sensitive to these
externalities. In part this was merely the result of having taken
up the issue later and of having absorbed the lesson of Europe's
growing preoccupation with the meteoric rise of U.S.-owned multi-
national business firms. Of course, these external actors--bap-
tized less reverently as "monopolios," "trustes," "explotaciones

1

yanquis"--had historically played a very prominent economic and
political role in the underdevelopment of the peripheral areas,
especially in Central and South America. Whether learned belatedly from the European experience or a result of the saliency
and visibility of external interference at home, both fears concerning external penetration and hopes relating to policy externalization were present from the beginning of regional integration
in Central America.[1]

Broadly speaking, one can identify three (not necessarily
mutually exclusive) "schools of thought" regarding the probable
external effects of Central American integration: the Marxist,
the Nationalist, and the Reformist. Each postulates the likelihood that "outsiders" (large North American and Western European
firms) will maneuver to appropriate many of the benefits of the
enlarged markets, but they differ as to the imputed motives of
the outsiders, the prospective outcome, and viable strategies of
resistance. None, needless to say, accepts permanently increased
external penetration as a desirable or inevitable by-product of
regional integration.

The Marxist critique sees regional trade liberalization,
in the absence of prior policy changes at the national level
(namely, socialization of the principal means of production and
distribution) and at the regional level (namely, creation of a
comprehensive, planned regional allocation of values), as simply
another "Trojan Horse of Imperialism." Foreign capitalists with
their greater financial power, prior multi-national articulation,
organizational flexibility, and entrepreneurial aggressiveness
would be in a commanding position to take advantage of the newly
created opportunities. They would quickly "cartelize" the region,
obviating any possible welfare benefits from greater competition
and/or economies of scale. In addition, their newly acquired
freedom to locate regardless of national restriction, due to the
removal of barriers to zonal trade, would permit them to play one
country off against another, thereby rendering ineffective any
attempts by individual "progressive" regimes to control their
activities.[2] The net product of such a negative or "liberal"

---

[1] Interest among intellectual observers within the region was
no doubt stimulated by the appearance in Spanish of François
Perroux's excellent and provocative essay "Quién integra? En
beneficio de quién se realiza la integración?," Revista de la
Integración, No. 1 (November 1967), pp. 9-39. For Central Americans this issue has been raised in Eduardo Lizano F., El Mercado
Común y la distribución del ingreso (San José: Editorial Universitaria Centroamericana, 1969).

[2] See Miguel Teubal, "The Failure of Latin America's Economic
Integration" in James Petras and Maurice Zeitlin, eds., Latin

integration movement would be to maximize the interdependencies between branches of extra-regional firms rather than to create a network of common goals and reciprocal interests between Central American polities. As such it would seem to represent a replication on a regional scale of the pattern of national <u>dis</u>integration created by liberal regimes and foreign interests in the nineteenth century--a prior stage in the subordinate incorporation of Central America into the capitalist system.

The Nationalist critique is based upon many of the same postulates, but tends to put more stress upon political variables and ideational motives. As stated by Celso Furtado,

> Such a regional "development project," which tends to render obsolete the idea of nationality as the principal political force in Latin America, offers many attractions to important sectors of the local ruling classes, who see in it an ingenious formula for deflating the "nationalism" which they hold responsible for most of the current social unrest. If most of the state's substantive functions in controlling the economic and social development process were taken away, countries would in all probability tend to diminish and government could then function principally on the "technical" level.[3]

While not opposed to regional integration as such (neither are the orthodox Marxists for that matter), the Nationalists emphasize its "prematurity." Individual Central American countries must first exploit their primary mobilizational resource--domestic nationalism--in independent efforts to recuperate national resources and redress existing assymetries in center-periphery relations. In the process, they will create stronger state institutions which will be more capable of participating equitably and self-confidently in regional political processes. Any integration movement which neglects or bypasses this prior national stage of political institutionalization and consciousness will

---

America: Reform or Revolution? (New York: Fawcett Books, 1968), pp. 120-144. This essay was originally published in 1965. For a more detailed and updated version, see Mauro Jiménez Lazcano, Integración económica e imperialismo (México: Editorial Nuestro Tiempo, 1968). For an early Communist treatment specifically of the Central American Common Market, see A. Guerra Borges and E. Mora Valverde, "Some Problems of the Economic Integration of Central America," World Marxist Review, 5 (June 1956), pp. 40-47.

[3]Celso Furtado, "U.S. Hegemony and the Future of Latin America" in Irving L. Horowitz et al., eds., Latin American Radicalism (New York: Vintage Books, 1969), pp. 72-73.

result in a weak set of regional organs unable to resist exploitation by giant foreign firms, manipulation by bureaucratic técnicos, and protracted tutelage by authoritarian rulers.[4] In short, the Nationalists are indirectly suggesting that premature regional integration in Latin America, rather than replicating the liberal pattern of the turn of the century, is much more likely to be analogous to the current pattern of national disintegration in Brazil--profoundly penetrated by external influences, incapable of elaborating an independent, assertive foreign policy, and suffering from depoliticized, bureaucratic-authoritarian rule.

The Reformist proponents of integration, most of them associated with either the Economic Commission for Latin America (ECLA) or the Institute for the Integration of Latin America (INTAL), have not ignored external effects, but they have not given them the prominence assigned to them by the other two "schools." In general, they concede that "mere" liberalization within a free trade zone will create differential benefits to the advantage of initially stronger external actors, and they use this probability to support their argument for the need for increasing both the scope and level of authority of new regional institutions. They tend to take an incrementalist position, however, pointing out that it is not possible to create these political capabilities de novo, but that they are likely to emerge only as the result of protracted interaction and negotiation among member-states. Gradually, with increased sensitivity to each other's problems, greater awareness of common objectives, and a wider variety of issues across which to "logroll," a harmonization of policy positions vis-à-vis the hegemonic external powers can be accomplished, and regional organizations can be used as instruments for elaborating a more forceful bargaining position in the world community. This, they argue, is simply the Central American version of a global process of regional bloc formation which cannot be resisted.[5]

---

[4]Ibid., pp. 61-74 passim.

[5]See Gustavo Lagos, International Stratification and Underdeveloped Countries (Chapel Hill, N.C.: University of North Carolina Press, 1963), pp. 66ff.; Victor L. Urquidi, Free Trade and Economic Integration in Latin America (Berkeley: University of California Press, 1962), pp. 115-117; Romulo Almeida et al., Factores para la integración latinoamericana (México: Fondo de Cultura Económica, 1966), esp. pp. 22-30, 64-68; Hélio Jaguaribe, "Coordinación de las políticas nacionales" in ibid., pp. 152-164; Miguel S. Wionczek, "Condiciones de una integración viable" in Wionczek, ed., Integración de América Latina (México: Fondo de Cultura Económica, 1964), pp. xviii-xxxi.

A related argument, advanced in the same circles, stresses the likelihood that an enlarged and protected regional market will serve to strengthen the confidence (and improve the fortunes) and thereby increase the assertiveness of the national industrial bourgeoisies. Eventually, these will combine (with state assistance) into authentically regional multi-national firms, capable of resisting or displacing those of extra-regional origin.[6]

It has been suggested that these two lines of "regional" causality will later merge. Stronger collective public institutions and more aggressive national private enterprises will trigger a general shift in political loyalties, and a new, more effective "continental nationalism" will emerge to replace or at least supplement existing but ineffective parochial nationalisms.[7]

Academic theorists of regional integration, especially of the neo-functional persuasion, initially ignored external causes and effects and only quite belatedly (and somewhat uncomfortably) have incorporated them within their analytical frameworks. Their tendency to stress internal unit characteristics arose, in part, as a reaction to prevailing international relations theories which treated sub-systemic integration as purely derivative from macro-systemic conditions. The external setting, according to these approaches, was the necessary and sufficient source for explaining and predicting the course of regional integration. Neo-functionalists, in particular, insisted on taking a less teleological and more actor-oriented approach which focused on perceived attitudes and interests. From this perspective, nation-states were best conceptualized not as unities obeying unconsciously the dictates of global homeostatic corrective mechanisms, but as congeries of classes, strata, sectors, and groups with differing interests engaging in a multiplicity of infra-national, national, and trans-national exchanges. Hence, there was a strong tendency to concentrate analysis upon these "internal" rates of transaction and degrees of interdependence

---

[6]José María Aragão, "Integración, dependencia y desarrollo: Reflexiones en torno de 'Sub-desarrollo y estancamiento en América Latina,'" Revista de la Integración, No. 1 (November 1967), pp. 105-126; Aldo Ferrer, "Empresario, integración y desarrollo," Los Empresarios y la integración de América Latina (Buenos Aires: INTAL, 1967), pp. 15-38; Marcos Kaplan, Problemas del desarrollo y de la integración en América Latina (Caracas: Monte Avila Editores, 1968), pp. 185-255.

[7]Felipe Herrera, Nacionalismo latinoamericano (Santiago: Editorial Universitaria, 1967), and Nacionalismo, regionalismo, internacionalismo (Buenos Aires: INTAL, 1970).

to the exclusion of those which bind actors to extra-regional
entities and systems.[8]

The "externalization hypothesis" served to focus explicit
attention on these neglected relationships by reminding the analyst that regional change processes are not autonomous or self-
generated, but responsive to a context of global interdependence
and interaction. In its original formulation, it suggested that

> once agreement is reached and made operative on a policy or
> set of policies pertaining to intermember or intraregional
> relations, participants will find themselves compelled--
> regardless of their original intentions--to adopt common
> policies vis-à-vis nonparticipant third parties. Members
> will be forced to hammer out a collective external position
> (and in the process are likely to have to rely increas-
> ingly on the new central institutions to do it).[9]

In an extensive revision of the hypothesis, I have sought
to relate external conditions more systematically to other regional change processes by means of a model based on crisis-induced
decisional cycles. In this revision,

> External conditions begin . . . as "givens." While the
> changes in national structures and values become at least
> partially predictable as consequences of regional decisions,
> the global dependence and client status of member states
> and the region as a whole continue to be exogenously deter-
> mined for a longer time. Nevertheless [by policy external-
> ization, these conditions] . . . will become less exogenously
> determined, if integrative rather than disintegrative strate-
> gies are commonly adopted. The "independent" role of these
> conditions should decline as integration proceeds until joint
> negotation vis-à-vis outsiders has become such an integral

---

[8]For a criticism of the literature on European integration for
ignoring the global setting, see Karl Kaiser, "The U.S. and the
EEC in the Atlantic System: The Problem of Theory," _Journal
of Common Market Studies,_ V (June 1967), pp. 388-425. This same
criticism has justifiably been leveled at the earlier theoretical
work of Ernst Haas and myself on Latin American integration. See
Joseph S. Nye, Jr., "Patterns and Catalysts in Regional Integration," _International Organization,_ XIX (Autumn 1965), pp. 870-
884, and Roger D. Hansen, "Regional Integration: Reflections on
a Decade of Theoretical Efforts," _World Politics,_ 21 (January
1969), pp. 257-270.

[9]Schmitter, "Three Neo-Functional Hypotheses about Regional
Integration," _International Organization,_ XXIII (Winter 1969),
p. 165. [IIS Reprint No. 329]

part of the decisional process that the [global] international-al system accords the new unit full participant status.[10]

The model suggests that the outcome of this dialectical encounter between increased dependence and policy externalization is partic-ularly sensitive to two regional change processes: (1) "the in-ternational status effect," or the extent to which the relative standing of individual countries or the region as a whole becomes perceived as dependent upon the comparative performance of its regional institutions, and (2) "regional reform-mongering," or the degree to which actors employed by or closely associated with the new regional institutions engage actively and deliberately in the promotion of new policies by anticipation--i.e., on the basis of intellectual or technical learning from analogous integration ex-periences before such measures are demanded or opposed by aroused interest representatives or threatened políticos. Other regional change processes which might contribute, positively or negatively, to either external penetration or policy externalization, are "re-gional group formation," "development of regional identity," and "equitability in the perceived distribution of benefits."[11]

The motives which might provide the impulse behind such processes are potentially multiple. First, national actors may simply transfer their successful collective experiences in other policy areas to the coordination of foreign policy. The original functionalist theories of integration placed a good deal of empha-sis on such learning of new habits by selected groups of experts and their surrounding interest clienteles.[12] Presumably, this re-quires either the physical circulation of such regionally enlight-ened elites from one policy arena to another or the less visible transfer of intellectual assessments from one elite to another.

There is a less visible motive which I have labelled else-where as "fall-out."[13] As regional integration proceeds, it tends

---

[10]"A Revised Theory of Regional Integration," International Organization, XXIV (Autumn 1970), p. 848. [IIS Reprint No. 364]

[11]Ibid., pp. 850ff.

[12]See David Mitrany, A Working Peace System (Chicago: Quad-rangle Books, 1966) and the discussion in Ernst B. Haas, Beyond the Nation-State (Stanford: Stanford University Press, 1964), pp. 12-13, 47-48, 79-85. Also Henry Teune, "The Learning of Integrative Habits" in P.E. Jacob and J.V. Toscano, eds., The Integration of Political Communities (Philadelphia: J.B. Lippin-cott, 1964), pp. 247-282.

[13]"Central American Integration: Spill-Over, Spill-Around or

to upset entrenched status and power relationships. At the national level, this may be reflected in changes at the cabinet or
budgetary level as actors engaged in the initial integration
policy areas acquire more resources or prestige. Foreign policy-
makers, left out of the original convergence, may seek to get in
on the act essentially to protect their domestic standing. Similarly, at the international level, successful negotiations by
other regional blocs will generate increased feelings of atimia,
or the desire to overcome peripheral status disparities, vis-à-
vis developed world centers. Simply to maintain (or improve)
their relative global standing, foreign policy-makers may resort
to greater regional collaboration.[14]

Yet another motive stressed by functionalist and neo-
functionalist theorists is well-summarized by the French expression engrenage. Decisions made on one issue are very likely to
impinge on others. Either bottlenecks will emerge which make it
impossible to obtain satisfaction in the original "preferred"
arena, or success in that arena will create new problems for
adjacent ones. While the degree of interdependence of the policy
matrix may vary according to the general level of structural differentiation of the economy and polity, everywhere it is likely
to generate internal tensions or contradictions which will impel
actors to reassess their respective integration strategies.[15]
No matter what their original intentions, it should prove difficult to isolate regional deliberations from their context of
global economic and political dependence.

Lastly and most obviously, regional actors may be forced
into policy externalization by the deliberate efforts of extra-
regional authorities and interests. By their very nature, regional integration movements are discriminatory. They establish
differential inducements for "insiders," and it is to be anticipated that "outsiders," especially hegemonic ones with superior

---

Encapsulation," Journal of Common Market Studies, IX, 1 (September
1970), pp. 32-37. [IIS Reprint No. 366]

[14]The sensitivity of foreign policy-makers in peripheral units
to such relative status calculations is suggestively explored in
Lagos. Johan Galtung has hypothesized that such incongruences
(or rank disequilibria) are more likely to conduce to aggressive,
rather than cooperative, behavior. See his "A Structural Theory
of Aggression," Journal of Peace Research, 2 (1964), pp. 95-119.

[15]This "crisis-ridden" view of integration processes, with its
emphasis on the distinction between exogenously produced tensions
and endogenously generated contradictions, is explored in my "A
Revised Theory of Regional Integration."

resources, will seek to mitigate if not eliminate such differen-
tials. Private external interests may seek to penetrate the new
reward system from within in an attempt to get inside the bound-
aries of the emerging regional system. Therefore, one can expect
that common market or free trade arrangements, in the absence of
deliberate restrictive policies, will stimulate flows of foreign
capital and technology. External public authorities may apply
several adaptive strategies. They may use openly obstructive
measures--e.g., refuse to recognize the authority of regionally
elaborated decisions, seek to invoke global or universalistic international norms, make separate and differential appeals in individual members, threaten reprisals. Should these fail to dis-
integrate the movement, or should the external power decide its
wider systemic interests will eventually be served by permitting
or even encouraging minor, sub-system forms of discrimination, it
may prefer penetrative to obstructive strategies. By aiding,
advising, subsidizing, cajoling, or flattering regional and national actors, outsiders may seek to influence the course of collaborative effort and thereby protect their "essential" interests
within the region. Either the obstructive or penetrative response
is likely to trigger policy externalization of differing degree
and type. The least "productive" external response is likely to
be indifference or indecision.

- - - -

Externalization processes represent not only a heretofore
ignored aspect of observer-elaborated theories, but also penetrate
to the core of actor-created ideologies of regional integration.
If, as the Marxist and Nationalist scenarios suggest, integration
movements at this point in time--with the varying types of political systems, levels of national consciousness, and degrees of
control over domestic resources--will merely provide an impetus
for penetration, then we can anticipate rising levels of popular
resistance to them and growing institutional paralysis within them.
If, on the other hand, the Reformist scenario is proven correct in
specifying certain dialectic qualities or countervailing tendencies
whereby these penetration effects stimulate an "equal and opposite
reaction" through policy externalization, not only will there be
some empirical support for their ideological position, but a new
and dynamic process relation will have been identified to add to
those already stressed by neo-functional theorists of integration.

In summary, then, regional integration has the (hypothet-
ically) paradoxical effect of encouraging "external penetration"
by private interests and public authorities at the same time that
it stimulates "policy externalization" by new regional institutions. Let us turn to a specific case--the Central American
Common Market (CACM)[16]--to see if we can find evidence of this

---

[16]The CACM is not technically a common market, but more closely

contradiction between those forces outside the region which seek
to control and subordinate the integration process to extra-
regional purposes and those forces within the region which seek
to use it to gain greater autonomy and bargaining power vis-à-vis
hegemonic outsiders. In the conclusion, we shall seek to assess
whether and how these two processes are linked and whether their
interaction tends to provoke concomitant change of an approximately equal magnitude.

---

resembles a customs union. For convenience' sake, however, I
will refer to it as the Common Market or by its Spanish acronym,
Mercomún.

Chapter 2

THE ROLE OF THE UNITED STATES IN
CENTRAL AMERICAN INTEGRATION

Central America well illustrates the extent to which a
region may be influenced by external forces and have only limited
mastery over a wide range of policy areas. One might even question the "external" status of the United States in this regional
subsystem.[17] Karl Deutsch argues that the existence of an analytical boundary between autonomous systems depends upon both
marked discontinuities in transactions, responses, and covariance,
and a certain degree of unpredictability of response "even from
the most thorough knowledge of the environment." Central America
barely fits the first system requisite (with Panama excluded),
but it is questionable whether national decision-makers possess
the second, "self-steering" capacity and whether their decisions
cannot be "commanded or reversed dependably from the environment."[18]

In the terminology of James Rosenau, the Central American
countries constitute clear cases of "penetrated political systems," in which "nonmembers of a national (or regional) society
participate directly and authoritatively, through actions taken
jointly with the society's members, in either the allocation of
its values or the mobilization of support on behalf of its
goals."[19] Rosenau's "pre-theoretical" and rather tautological

---

[17]For example, consider the following apologetic understatement
from a recent work on the history of United States-Latin American
relations: "It was after the turn of the century, when the
Caribbean became a focal point of American diplomacy, that the
American government adopted a policy of active participation in
the promotion of Central American peace and stability, a policy
which inevitably increased the influence of the United States in
the internal affairs of these countries" (J. Lloyd Mecham, A
Survey of United States-Latin American Relations [Boston:
Houghton Mifflin, 1965], p. 335).

[18]"External Influences on the Internal Behavior of States" in
R. Barry Farrell, ed., Approaches to Comparative and International
Politics (Evanston: Northwestern University Press, 1966), pp.
5-7.

[19]"Pre-Theories and Theories of Foreign Policy" in ibid., p. 65.

11

observation is that small, underdeveloped, and penetrated societies, with either open or closed polities, are especially vulnerable in their foreign policy-making to "systemic" constraints--i.e., to the nonhuman environment and/or the acts of outside political actors. More recently, Rosenau has characterized the resultant policy outcome as one of "acquiescent adaptation," in which "officials perceive themselves, accurately or not, as lacking the capacity to alter or offset the demands (usually of the nearest superpower), and thus they are not inclined to bargain with those who make them."[20] In short, it could be argued that at the initiation of its integration process, few regions of the globe exhibited higher levels of external penetration and lower levels of policy externalization than Central America.

A Brief Historical Synopsis[21]

Although the history of the five Central American republics--Costa Rica, El Salvador, Guatemala, Honduras, and Nicaragua--has been punctuated by a succession of attempts (most forceful) at reconstituting the unity imposed by the colonial Captaincy-General of Guatemala, not until 1951 was a permanent institutional forum for joint decision-making established. In that year, in fact, two organizations were founded: the Central American Committee for Economic Cooperation (CCE) and the Organization of Central American States (ODECA).

While the latter, more overtly political effort vegetated, the former, economic one prospered. By a series of bilateral and then multilateral agreements, culminating in the General Treaty of Managua (1960), the Five accepted higher and higher levels of mutual obligation and widened the scope of their collective deliberations.

The General Treaty of 1960 was not simply a once-and-for-all agreement to eliminate barriers on mutual trade or to

---

[20]"The Adaptation of National Societies: A Theory of Political System Behavior and Transformation" (New York: McCaleb-Seiler, 1970), p. 7.

[21]This summary of the history and institutional structure of the Central American integration movement is adapted from my article "Central American Integration: Spill-Over, Spill-Around or Encapsulation?" A more comprehensive introductory description can be found in James D. Cochrane, The Politics of Regional Integration: The Central American Case (New Orleans: Tulane University Press, 1969).

distribute benefits according to some pre-established formula, but a rather ingeniously contrived set of continuous obligations to meet recurrently in the elaboration of a number of interrelated endeavors. Over a period of five years, the members were to negotiate the removal of almost all of the exceptions to free regional trade and the formation of a common external tariff. Within six months to one year, they were to agree upon the following: establishing and operating a regional development bank; protocols fixing the identity, location, and performance of "integration industries"; a treaty establishing uniform fiscal incentives for industrial development; mutual consultations before signing any future treaties affecting regional free trade; and a Central American Standard Customs Code. There was no guarantee that agreement would be reached in these endeavors, least of all within the stipulated time-period, but at least there was a definite commitment to the continued participation of an increasing variety of national actors in joint deliberations.

The 1960 Treaty did not delegate manifestly "supranational" powers to a regional agency, although it did provide for some important institutional innovations. Three permanent bodies were established: the Central American Economic Council, formed by the five Ministers of Economy; the Executive Council, composed of "one titular official and one alternate" appointed by each country; and a Permanent Secretariat (SIECA), with headquarters in Guatemala City and a secretary-general appointed for a three-year term. None of these three was subordinated to any existing regional organization, and only the most tenuous of relations linked their efforts with those of ODECA or other regional organizations, such as the Central American Defense Council (CONDECA), the Superior University Council of Central America (CSUCA), or the Nutrition Institute of Central America and Panama (INCAP).

The latent, if not manifest, spirit of the Central American economic agreement lay in the provision of an institutional framework, a set of interrelated policy instruments, and a continuous, virtually open-ended commitment to joint deliberation in order to tackle the imbalances in benefits and the disparities in objectives which the drafters of the agreement anticipated would arise. It was a regional treaty based not on the harmonious exploitation of consensus, but at least potentially upon the creative manipulation of conflict. (This potential for conflict manipulation was totally lacking in the Treaty of Montevideo which founded the Latin American Free Trade Area [LAFTA].) The original Central American convergence of actor purposes and strategies was silent on the issue of externalization. No specific obligations (except on the harmonization of fiscal incentives designed to attract foreign capital) were undertaken; no agreed-upon modalities of collective response to the fully anticipated (and desired) increase in external penetration were suggested; no institutions were specifically charged with policy externalization.

All this was left (implicitly) to the "creative manipulation" of imbalance, dissatisfaction, and conflict.

Elsewhere I have analyzed in detail the subsequent (1960-69) performance of these Common Market institutions by issue area. I concluded that, unlike previous integrative syndromes, there was little evidence of cumulative expansion in both the scope and level of regional authority (the "spill-over" pattern) or of a wholesale retraction (as of 1969) in both dimensions, whereby regional organizations lose previously acquired capacities (the "spill-back" pattern):

> Nevertheless, some sort of expansive logic seems to be operating, but not for the reasons stressed or with the consequences predicted by the neo-functionalist argument. Regional actors have not simply confined themselves to their originally assigned tasks, and sealed themselves off from perturbing external forces--a syndrome . . . called self-encapsulation. The global impression is less one of inter-sectorial clashes rooted in underlying interdependence, than one of conscious differentiation into distinct arenas, each with its own set of obligations, style and decision-making, rhythm of progress and attitudes toward integration. The task expansion which has occurred has rarely been generated by expressed dissatisfaction, mobilized group interest or 'learned' generalizations from past experience. In only one case (planning) has it resulted in the accretion of new functions or the delegation of new decisional authority to a single set of central regional institutions.

> To describe the Central American response pattern more accurately, I . . . propose a new concept: 'spill-around', a sort of composite or hybrid of the spill-over and self-encapsulation syndromes. It is characterized by a pro-liferation of independent efforts at regional coordination in distinct functional spheres--i.e., an expansion in the scope of regional tasks--without, however, a concomitant devolution of authority to a single collective body--i.e., without an increase in the level of regional decision-making. New issue areas become 'collectivized' or 'regionalized' and transaction rates increase impressively, but there is no transcendence, no fundamental redefinition of norms and goals, no development of a supranational political process, no emergence of a new and wider sense of community loyalty. The new institutions sprout up or are revitalized in a more or less uncoordinated manner. Each is relatively autonomous from the other, depending upon different sources of national political and financial support, as well as external aid and encouragement in the Central American case. The expansionist logic of the spill-around process is not based on the presence of functional interdependence

14

between actors and problem areas, as is the case of the other syndromes.[22]

In arriving at this assessment, I paid relatively little attention to the activities of, or reactions to, external actors as they sought to profit from or directly influence regional processes. This intrinsically conflictive and mutually determinate (dialectic, if you will) relationship between external penetration and policy externalization is the central focus of this complementary effort on my part at understanding the process of Central American integration.

External Penetration

Despite the absence of prior agreement on how to deal with them, external actors were present from the start of Central American integration. Although our preoccupation in this essay is with process--i.e., the subsequent course of events--it is important to note certain general features of the global international setting of the mid- and late-1950's which encouraged the initiation of the Mercomún. The "hegemonic alliance" encouraged and imposed by the United States protected the region from competitive cold-war or neutralist options and enforced a substantial degree of political orthodoxy, despite some major differences in regime type among the Five. The substantial role of international economic institutions, especially the International Monetary Fund (IMF) and the World Bank (IBRD) ensured a considerable fidelity to common principles of monetary and budgetary orthodoxy and "free enterprise" capitalist development. A secular trend toward declining terms-of-trade which set in after the end of the Korean War and persistent irregularity in the world demand and prices for its limited export items--agricultural raw materials--had begun to upset traditional policy arrangements, and limited greatly the possibilities for a return to the "outward oriented" development strategies of the past. In addition, the perceived success of the recently organized European Economic Community stimulated the continuing desire of Central American elites "to look modern"--in this case, to keep up with modern trends in international law and organization. Finally, the pervasive fear of Castroite subversion after 1959 added a desperate sense of urgency, making elites much more willing to experiment with policy innovations, especially ones which seemed to promise popular returns at no cost to established privileges and perquisites.

This peculiar concatenation of penetrative elements in the late 1950's undoubtedly facilitated a regionalist response.

---

[22]"Central American Integration," p. 39.

The Economic Commission for Latin America (ECLA) and the United States provided additional positive inducements for such a response. Whether the project would have ever been conceived without the ideological and theoretical support of the former, or whether the negotiative brinkmanship of 1960 would have been successful without the financial "carrot-dangling" of the latter, is doubtful but indeterminable.[23]

Foreign Trade

A recent essay critical of the Central American Common Market (CACM) suggests that one of its unacknowledged founding purposes may have been to protect a declining U.S. trade position. The region's traditionally high and assymetric dependence on imports from and exports to the United States had begun to waiver in the aftermath of the Korean War. European and Japanese traders were beginning to intrude and to threaten the hitherto uncontested U.S. hegemony. The emerging customs union arrangement of the CACM would encourage import-substitution in conditions especially favorable to industrial investment in plants using U.S. semi-elaborated imports and capital equipment.[24] The structure of Central America's imports might change, but the U.S. proportion of it would grow or, at the least, remain constant. Since the importation of this new type of goods would be more intimately related to domestic employment, savings, and investment than previous imports, thereby making them more difficult to curtail, external penetration would increase, even if the global quantum of trade did not.

---

[23]For the argument that ECLA inspiration was necessary and the U.S. role catalytic, see Joseph S. Nye, Jr., "Central American Regional Integration," International Conciliation, No. 562 (March 1967), p. 52. J. Abraham Bennaton, a participant in the crucial tripartite negotiations and currently Deputy Secretary-General of SIECA, has given a detailed account of the events which places decisive emphasis on the role of the Frank-Turkel U.S. State Department Mission, which reportedly promised a $100 million payoff and even encouraged El Salvador and Honduras to proceed bilaterally if necessary (El Mercado Común Centroamericano: Su evolución y perspectivas [Tegucigalpa: Tesis, Universidad Autónoma de Honduras, Facultad de Ciencias Económicas, Septiembre 1964], pp. 100-103). However, neither Cepalinos nor North Americans participated directly in the drafting and, in Paragraph 7 of the "Declaración de Esquipulas," the parties proclaimed their willingness to proceed "even if external aid is lacking."

[24]David Tobis, "The Central American Common Market: The Integration of Underdevelopment," NACLA Newsletter, III (January 1970), p. 4.

Table 1

NORTH AMERICAN TRADE WITH CENTRAL AMERICA: 1950-1968

	1950	1955	1958	1961	1964	1965	1966	1967	1968
Imports from U.S. and Canada as Percentage of Total Central American Imports	73.1	64.4	57.1	48.5	51.8	42.8	42.8	41.4	38.9
Exports to U.S. and Canada as Percentage of Total Central American Exports	--	62.4	53.4	50.8	36.1	37.4	37.4	34.8	32.8

Sources: International Monetary Fund, International Financial Statistics; SIECA, Indicadores económicos centroamericanos, Nos. 8-9 (January 1970).

The data in Table 1 indicate that, regardless of the
imputed intention, the implementation of the CACM has been concomitant with a proportional decline in the U.S. overall trading
position, especially as regards exports. Of course, these figures
conceal the qualitative change which has occurred in the nature
of imports, and the probability that much of the growing intra-
Central American trade is attributable to branches of U.S. firms.
Nevertheless, regional trade liberation has not impeded Central
America from diversifying its sources of external supply and
demand.[25] In this restricted sense, integration--while not
lessening dependence (in fact, extra-zonal foreign trade as a
percentage of zonal GNP has increased)--has distributed it a bit
more broadly.

Foreign Investment

No one (to my knowledge) has suggested that the integration movement was inspired or initiated by foreign capitalists.[26]
No one, however, can dispute that they have prospered in its
wake. As Table 2 indicates, the total book value of U.S. investments grew impressively--almost twice as rapidly from 1960 to 1965
(40 percent) as from 1955 to 1960 (22 percent). This is a higher
rate of increase than for U.S. investment in Latin America as a
whole, or for domestic investment within Central America. Additional evidence of the impact of the new regional reward system
can be gleaned from the marked change in the sectoral composition
of foreign capital. Granted that the shift from public utilities
and agriculture into manufacturing antedated slightly the effective application of the General Treaty and had been occurring
elsewhere as well, most observers credit trade liberalization and
market expansion with having attracted external funds to this
sector. A large share of these have gone into new consumer-
oriented "assembly industries" and petroleum refining, both of
which use high quotients of imported inputs and tend to complement
existing domestic industries rather than compete with them for
raw materials or customers. Nonetheless, some of these domestic,
quasi-artisanal enterprises have begun to feel the competition of
assembly-line manufacturing and product specialization, and there
have been a number of well-publicized cases of such industries

---

[25]Of course, it is possible that much of Central America's new
trade with Europe involves U.S. subsidiaries located there, but
this is not likely to be the case with Japan.

[26]Nor, I might add, has anyone argued convincingly that domestic
capitalists had much of a say in its initiation.

Table 2

U.S. DIRECT PRIVATE INVESTMENT IN CENTRAL AMERICA: 1955-1968

Sector	1955 US$ (millions)	1955 Percent Distribution	1960 US$ (millions)	1960 Percent Distribution	1965 US$ (millions)	1965 Percent Distribution	1968 US$ (millions)	1968 Percent Distribution
Mining	15	4.9	20	5.3	35	6.8	241	29.2
Petroleum	40	13.0	50	13.3	140	26.6	121	15.2
Manufacturing	2	0.7	15	4.0	56	10.6	121	15.2
Public Utilities	95	30.9	126	33.5	127	24.1	146	18.4
Commerce	10	3.3	16	4.3	27	5.1	44	5.6
Other (including Agriculture)	145	47.2	149	39.6	141	26.8	243	30.6
Total	307	100.0	376	100.0	526	100.0	795	100.0

Sources: For 1955, 1960, 1965: Gert K. Rosenthal, "Algunos apuntes sobre la inversión extranjera directa en el Mercado Común Centroamericano," INTAL, Sem. 11/dt. 6, 17 November 1969; for 1968: David Tobis, "The Central American Common Market: The Integration of Under- development," NACLA Newsletter, III (January 1970). In both cases, the original source was U.S. Department of Commerce, Survey of Current Business. US$ figures for 1968 by sector are my calculations based on Tobis' total and percentage data.

selling out to foreign interests.[27] In his case-study of Guatemala (incidentally, the only one which does not rely exclusively on U.S.-supplied data), Gert Rosenthal documents in great detail a similar pattern: preponderance of U.S. interests (90 percent of all new foreign investment); marked concentration in light manufacturing (increase from 10 to 33 percent in the period 1963-68); increase relative to domestic investment (from 14.5 in 1965 to 17.1 percent of total investment in 1968); very low levels of local "participation" (over one half the foreign firms had no national capital at all); increasingly high rates of profit re-investment, but even more rapidly increasing rates of profit remittance abroad; and extensive dependence on imported inputs (34.5 percent of total sales value). Despite these not very encouraging trends, Rosenthal concludes optimistically that the Guatemalan evidence does not support "the image of multinational firms sending high profits back home, based on a meagre investment and low value-added to imported raw materials." He further notes that foreign industrial capital at the most represents 20 percent of all industrial capital investment and is not, therefore, "dominant," and that the buying-out of national firms may have had salutary effects on employment and production.[28]

Rosenthal, however, does not mention another important area of external penetration: the replacement of private national banks by branches of large U.S. banks and the proliferation

---

[27]Carlos Castillo, Growth and Integration in Central America (New York: Praeger, 1966), pp. 100-102; Evaluación de la integración económica en Centroamérica (New York: U.N., ECLA, 1966), pp. 56-59; Roger D. Hansen, Central America: Regional Integration and Economic Development (Washington, D.C.: National Planning Association, 1967), pp. 42-43. For an intelligent critique of the impact of regional trade liberalization on industrialization, see Sidney Dell, "Obstacles to Latin American Integration" in R. Hilton, ed., The Movement Toward Latin American Unity (New York: Praeger, 1969), pp. 64-65. Dell concludes that "integration would appear to run much more strongly from the subsidiaries to the parent companies than between the countries participating in the tariff reduction program."

[28]"Algunos apuntes sobre la inversión extranjera directa en el Mercado Común Centroamericano," mimeo document, INTAL (Buenos Aires), Sem. 11/dt. 6, 17 November 1969. The ECLA Evaluación arrives at a similar conclusion: "Despite the moderate increase registered during the last two years, the situation in Central America is not of an excess, rather--on the contrary--a scarcity of direct industrial investment of foreign origin" (p. 58).

of U.S.-run mutual funds and investment firms.[29] This, coupled
with the developments in the industrial sector, has lent considerable credence to the view that, although inspired by the principle
of regional self-affirmation, the practice of Central American
integration has been fundamentally alienative. At worst, it
seems to have established a new schedule of incentives which
discriminates in favor of foreign capitalists; at best it seems
to have failed to provide domestic interests with sufficient
protection against the superior exploitative capacity of outside
competitors. Either way, the new regional arrangements have
stimulated penetration by external private interests to such an
extent that two of the few remaining areas of national decisional
autonomy--native industry and domestic finance--seem threatened.
Before looking for the policy responses (or non-responses) to
this "successful" process, let us look briefly at external public
or governmental attempts to affect and control the integration
movement.

External Public Actors

The U.S. government, by far the preponderant public
authority in Central America's external environment, has historically been opposed to the economic integration of the region.
In the first decades of this century, it maneuvered successfully
to kill two such attempts and insisted on circumventing embryonic
regional institutions and dealing bilaterally with the five countries.[30] In 1958, it publicly reversed this policy and declared:
"We have supported a free trade area in Central America. We have
also made it clear that we are prepared, through the Export-Import
Bank, to consider dollar financing required by regional industries
in Latin America."[31] This relative U.S. abstention (or indecision)

---

[29] See Miguel S. Wionczek, "U.S. Investment and the Development
of Middle America: A Latin American Viewpoint," paper presented
at the Conference on Western Hemisphere International Relations
and the Caribbean Area, Kingston, Jamaica, May 16-18, 1968--pp.
11ff. and works cited therein.

[30] For a succinct, but well documented account, see S. Lorenzo
Harrison, "Central American Dilemma: National Sovereignty or
Unification," International Review of History and Political
Science, 2 (December 1965), pp. 100-110.

[31] C. Douglas Dillon, "An Integrated Program of Development for
Latin America," Department of State Bulletin, XXXIX (December 8,
1958), p. 921, as cited in Cochrane. Cochrane caustically observes that the Department of State simultaneously claimed that
it had "given its advice and moral support" for an unspecified

in the pre-1960 formative period was probably beneficial: it gave the integration movement at the start an authentically autochthonous image.[32]

Once the United States had decided to support the Central American Common Market, however, it did so unambiguously and energetically.[33] Verbal encouragement was backed up with material inducement and organizational innovation. For the first time a special field agency--the Regional Office for Central America and Panama (ROCAP)--was set up to provide "a coordinating point for the planning and administration of AID-supported regional programs." In effect, the U.S. was informally (and prematurely) "recognizing" the emerging regional organizations,[34] manifesting

---

prior period of time--but that he (nor I) found no evidence of this from 1951 to 1958. Milton S. Eisenhower's trip through the region seems to have played a key role in this policy change; see his The Wine is Bitter (Garden City, N.Y.: Doubleday, 1963).

[32]"The preliminary stage consisted of building up local technical elites, politically neutral but convinced of a need for regional economic cooperation. The education of such elites was left to Central American regional institutions, created for that purpose and manned in the great majority by the Central Americans and by "neutral" foreigners, mainly other Latin Americans. Consequently, at no point during the preparatory work for a regional cooperation mechanism could charges have been made that the scheme was managed, inspired, or abetted from outside, although no one can deny that Central America has been, since the last quarter of the nineteenth century, in the direct zone of influence of the United States. Fortunately for the experiment itself, the United States was not interested in the scheme until 1959. When at that moment it offered financial support for integration, the groundwork had already been laid" (Wionczek, "Latin American Integration and United States Economic Policies" in R.W. Gregg, ed., International Organization in the Western Hemisphere (Syracuse: Syracuse University Press, 1968), p. 96.

[33]Contrary to its vacillating posture vis-à-vis the Latin American Free Trade Area. See Robert E. Denham, "The Role of the U.S. as an External Actor in the Integration of Latin America," Journal of Common Market Studies, VII (March 1969), pp. 199-216; also Wionczek, "Latin American Integration," pp. 125-143.

[34]ROCAP officials are not directly accredited to SIECA or other CACM institutions (as are diplomatic officials to the Bruxelles Commission of EEC), but are legally part of the U.S.-AID mission to Guatemala. ROCAP, however, operates as an independent agency. For an interesting history of ROCAP, see U.S. House of Represen-

openly its sympathy with the program, and establishing the institutional basis for a special supportive relationship bypassing bilateral channels. By 1969, ROCAP had distributed some U$S 112.5 million, most of which had gone to the Central American Integration Bank (CABEI) for infrastructural and industrial projects, as well as research and feasibility studies.[35] In its formative years, AID-ROCAP funds even paid the Bank's administrative overhead. With 55 of its U$S 67 million capitalization (as of 1968) coming from the U.S., CABEI is--to put it mildly-- a heavily subsidized institution. Through it the predominant external actor has its greatest direct impact upon the economic integration process. All loans over a minimal size must be approved by ROCAP and Washington.[36] The most obvious case in which this financial leverage has been exercised concerned the long-standing prohibition on the use of CABEI loans to support so-called "integration industries."[37] While there have been to date

---

tatives, Committee on Foreign Affairs, Subcommittee on Inter-American Affairs, Central America: Some Observations on Its Common Market, Binational Centers and Housing Programs (Washington, D.C.: Government Printing Office, August 4, 1966), pp. 24-27.

[35]The decision to establish ROCAP and support multilateral regional organizations did not, however, mean any dismantling of bilateral channels or programs. From 60 to 80 percent of U.S. public funding to Central America went directly for national projects, few of which made any "regional" contribution and some of which could be considered alternatives to a more concerted, multilateral developmental strategy. From interviews (in 1967) I gathered considerable evidence of tension between ROCAP ("over-staffed and separate") and the national AID missions ("parochial and ill-informed"). There is no evidence that the U.S. has consciously sought to promote regional solutions by cutting back the funding on national ones, although from Table 4 (see p. 32 below) one might infer that bilateral flows were bankrolling side-payments to integration losers.

[36]Raymond Mikesell has observed that the need for ROCAP and Washington approval lengthens the decisional circuit by as much as five months ("External Financing and Regional Integration" in Wionczek, ed., Latin American Economic Integration [New York: Praeger, 1966], p. 213). All projects involving loans over $500,000 must take this lengthy route.

[37]See Wionczek, "Experiences of the Central American Economic Integration Program as Applied to East Africa," Industrialization and Productivity, 11 (1968), pp. 14-22. Also Cochrane, "U.S. Attitudes Towards Central American Economic Integration," Inter-

no publicized cases of clashes over loan approvals, there is no way of calculating how many projects were not presented by native entrepreneurs or not promoted by regional officials in anticipation of U.S. opposition. In any case, the close supervision by AID (and, once removed, the U.S. Congress) has certainly contributed to the conservativeness of the Bank's lending policy and the timidity with which it has dealt with the issue of "regional" loans going to predominantly extra-regional capitalists.

Nor does the U.S. penetration of regional institutions stop there. ROCAP has also provided SIECA with direct financial support.[38] According to interviews and some documentary evidence, ROCAP-SIECA relations have changed considerably over time. Originally, there was a certain méfiance, if not hostility, between the two--reflecting, no doubt, the policy differences between the U.S. government and ECLA. SIECA informants complained of the aggressiveness and rigidity with which U.S. representatives pushed objectives of free market competition, development of the private sector, and foreign investment, and opposed attempts at planning and extension of state controls; the early ROCAP officials (there were only five to start with) seemed to regard the Cepalinos as unrealistic and naive bureaucrats, bent on complete domination of the movement.

There were, however, a number of areas in which interests were convergent, and ROCAP began funding specific projects within SIECA, such as the development of a statistical capacity, elaboration of economic indicators, industrial censuses, customs nomenclature, and tariff administration. The scope and intensity of U.S. support began to shift after 1964. Indirectly, through the OAS and the IADB, U.S. funds were used to create and maintain the Joint Planning Mission, and subsequently a special allocation financed its incorporation within SIECA. Currently there is a request in its "pipeline" from SIECA for U$S 50 million to support the research and organizational costs of the forthcoming negotiations with LAFTA.

ROCAP officials are quite aware, not only that they have been channeling an increasing quantity of funds through SIECA, but that the quality of their contribution has been changing.

American Economic Affairs, 18 (Autumn 1964), pp. 84 et seq. U.S. opposition to the scheme has since softened, and Nicaragua's integration industry (a caustic soda plant, mostly U.S.-owned) has received loans from CABEI and IADB.

[38] According to Nye's calculations, about one-fifth of SIECA's 1966 operating budget came frm U.S.-AID sources (Nye, "Central American Regional Integration," p. 35).

From the originally "technical," they have been becoming increasingly "political"--straight budgetary support (usually
limited to two years) in areas of policy initiative. In the
words of a high ROCAP official (in an interview with the author
in 1967):

> Formerly our assistance was confined to statistics and
> custom harmonization studies, and there was not much pos-
> sibility for leverage in these areas. Now that they are
> in a financial bind, we are getting into other areas.
> Here ROCAP can, and we intend to, exercise more overall
> strategic leverage--by earmarking funds for specific tasks
> and insisting on their setting priorities.

The implications of this qualitative change are by no
means lost on the regional técnicos. They insist that the ROCAP
support is marginal (but very useful) and that SIECA could easily
survive a withdrawal of it should a major policy clash occur.
Despite the increasing interpenetration and encroachment on
sensitive issues, SIECA-ROCAP relations are good. Both parties
stress that the other has grown more flexible and tolerant--in
short, there is evidence of a typical integrative learning sequence at work. One important aspect of the relationship is
ROCAP's leaving the initiative to the regional secretariat and
limiting itself to incremental modifications. It does not seek
to push projects or objections directly upon SIECA--as it has done
in some of the other regional organizations. As one U.S. official reported to me in 1967:

> ROCAP is not used as a protest channel, only as an informa-
> tion channel. We leave most of that to the embassies and
> commercial attachés in the individual countries. If we
> were, for example, to protest against the regulation of
> foreign capital to SIECA, it would ruin our relations with
> them.

But SIECA is not the only recipient of U.S. aid; virtually
every regional organization receives funds from U.S. public
sources.[39] Some of this antedates the signing of the General
Treaty--e.g., the Central American Institute of Research and Industrial Technology (ICAITI) and the Institute of Nutrition of
Central America and Panama (INCAP); some of it has been contracted
since then--e.g., the Central American School of Public Administration (ESAPAC), the Central American Institute of Public
Administration (now ICAP), the Superior University Council of
Central America (CSUCA), and the Central American Air Navigation
Services Corporation (COCESNA). The most important "external"

---

[39]Ibid.

decision came in 1964, however, when the U.S. began to allocate
a substantial amount of support to an almost prostrate ODECA.
This might be interpreted as a strategy on its part to compensate
for its inability to control SIECA by creating an institutional
counterweight and, thereby, to prevent the latter's gaining a
complete monopoly of the integration process. According to
ROCAP and ODECA officials, there was no such ulterior strategic
purpose. A convergence of two factors--a new head of ROCAP more
sensitive to the multivariate nature of the integration process,
and a new head of ODECA anxious to expand the activity of his
organization--led to the decision. ODECA now receives more than
one half of its operating expenses from AID. Unlike SIECA (and
CABEI), who have been able to squeeze additional contributions
out of member governments, virtually all of ODECA's expanded
activity has been externally financed.

Programs in social, education, and demographic statistics;
studies in manpower, employment, and social security; research
in public health and coordination of malaria eradication; revision
of legal curricula and publication of a regional legal compendium;
writing, printing, and circulation of regionally uniform school-
books--all this has become the mainstay of ODECA, and it is all
U.S.-financed. While it is difficult to measure the direct impact of this upon regional integration (and impossible to estimate
its indirect contribution),[40] the immediate effect has been to
create something of a rival integrative center. Actually, when
one examines in detail how the funds are allocated and disbursed,
one discovers that their impact is even more decentralizing.
ODECA functions simply as a convenient, but impotent, "umbrella"
(to use the expression of a high ROCAP official), and actual support goes directly to its independent councils (Health, Education,
Labor, etc.) or departments. In short, U.S. aid has been under-
writing a vast process of institutional proliferation at the
regional level.

In one sector in particular, this compartmentalization
of the integration process has been very marked--the military.
Of course, this is due in good measure to the fact that, as one
respondent commented, "the military in these countries live in

---

[40]Mikesell observes that "activities sponsored by AID's Regional
Organization for Central America and Panama . . . appear to be
content with providing approximately equal and standardized services for the five Central American states rather than lending
support to regional integration" (Mikesell, p. 212). However, one
can make a persuasive argument that such an equalization and
standardization of capacities and information is indirectly conducive to integration, if not a requisite for it.

their own world." It is also a reflection of the fact that the
U.S. military's external assistance program seems to operate in
its own world.[41]

Efforts to increase cooperation between the area's military forces began formally with the First Meeting of Central
American Defense Ministers in 1956, and appear to have been
inspired by Guatemalan fears of an exile invasion. Except for
a follow-up meeting of a special commission in 1957, international
rivalries prevented any further collective action. The coming
to power of Fidel Castro supplied the precipitating factor. The
revised Charter of ODECA (1962) contained a provision for a Central American Defense Council (CONDECA), and the following year,
Guatemala, Honduras, and Nicaragua signed the treaty creating it.
El Salvador has since joined; Costa Rica sends observers; Panama
has recently begun to participate in some of its activities.[42]

Military integration (CONDECA officials prefer the term
unification) got started late and has advanced slowly in Central
America. As the New York Times observed in 1961 when the Chiefs
of Staff met for the first time, "Each country, due to a series
of changes in political alliances and economic pressures, sus-
pected the other as possible sources of invasion to their respective territories."[43] Despite this, several joint maneuvers have
been held; a permanent secretariat has been established (the
Permanent Commission of CONDECA); an intelligence service has
been created to exchange information on the movements of each
other's "subversives"; plans have been drafted for mutual assistance in the event of invasion; some progress has been made in
the standardization of internal organization, systems of mobilization, equipment, and training. Nevertheless, according to an
interview with a CONDECA official, policies of military purchasing
remain exclusively nationally determined, and the unification of
officer training schools is still in the planning stage.

Force levels in Central America have remained relatively
constant since the debut of CONDECA, but total expenditures and,

---

[41]For a discussion of Presidential attempts to remind U.S.
ambassadors in the field that they were empowered to supervise
the operations of U.S. military missions, see Harold A. Hovey,
United States Military Assistance: A Study of Policies and
Practices (New York: Praeger, 1965), pp. 56-57.

[42]Panama and Costa Rica officially have no armies. In 1966
the CONDECA charter was revised to permit participation of
"Ministers of National Security," opening the door to full participation of these two countries.

[43]NYT, October 29, 1961.

especially, expenditures per member of the armed forces have increased sharply[44]--in large part as a result of the acceptance by the military establishments of a new strategy of military security emphasizing counter-insurgency and civic action.

The major proponent of this revised role for Latin American militaries has been the United States. Particularly with the shift in control over military assistance in Latin America to the U.S. Southern Command in the Canal Zone in the early 1960's, considerable incentives were offered to (and, one suspects, strong pressures brought to bear on) the Central American countries to coordinate their defense efforts. It was the United States which brought Honduras, Guatemala, Nicaragua, and Perú together for the crucial "Operación Fraternidad" in 1962, and which supported subsequent joint maneuvers in 1965 and 1966. Table 3 shows a very substantial increase in U.S. military aid to Central America since the formation of CONDECA. If the figures are comparable, they suggest that more U.S. military support was given to Central America in the three years from 1962 to 1965 than in the preceeding twelve! The externally supplied proportion of the military budgets of Central American countries increased astronomically between 1960 and 1964, and virtually all of this consisted of outright grants. The North American military missions in these countries continue to be relatively small (despite reports of heavy U.S. involvement in Guatemala); however, the external impact on training has been substantial, which is perhaps best gauged by the number of Central Americans taking courses in the "Escuela de las Americas," a counter-insurgency school in the Canal Zone, and the Army Special Warfare Center in Fort Bragg, North Carolina. According to Barber and Ronning, almost 50 percent (8,154) of the Canal Zone's 16,343 graduates from 1961 to 1964 were Central Americans.[45]

The external--i.e., United States--impact on integration in this sector has been very great, if not determinate. Inter-

---

[44]See Joseph E. Loftus, "Latin American Defense Expenditures, 1938-1965," RAND Memorandum, RM-5310-PR/ISA (January 1968). It should be noted that overall governmental expenditures have also risen sharply during the integration period. Hence, as a percent of the total budget, military expenditures have not risen dramatically. In fact, they have declined proportionately in El Salvador, Honduras, and Nicaragua. It would be erroneous, therefore, to assume that military integration has caused a decisive shift in domestic resource allocation in favor of the armed forces.

[45]W. Barber and C.N. Ronning, International Security and Military Power (Columbus: Ohio State University Press, 1966), p. 149.

Table 3

U.S. MILITARY ASSISTANCE TO CENTRAL AMERICA: 1950-1968

Total U.S. Military Aid (in U$S millions)	Guatemala	El Salvador	Honduras	Nicaragua	Costa Rica
1950-1962[a]	$ 4.3	$1.1	$2.3	$ 3.8	$0.8
1950-1968[b]	13.1	5.3	6.4	10.2	1.8
Increase: 1962-1968	8.9	4.2	4.1	6.4	1.0
U.S. Military Aid as Percentage of Country Defense Effort					
1960[a]	2.8%	1.7%	3.3%	6.6%	3.7%
1964[c]	14.5	10.9	7.5	13.7	11.4

Sources: [a]John D. Powell, "Military Assistance and Militarism in Latin America," Western Political Quarterly, Vol. XVIII (June 1965), p. 385.

[b]U.S. Department of Defense, Office of the Assistant Secretary of Defense for International Security Affairs, Military Assistance Facts (Washington, D.C., 1969), pp. 16-17.

[c]Hovey, p. 65.

viewees in CONDECA, although insistent that their efforts were Central American-inspired and controlled, acknowledged that contacts with the Inter-American Defense Board and the U.S. Southern Command, as well as with the U.S. military missions in each country, were frequent and intimate. Military "unification" is certainly not the only U.S. security objective in the area,[46] but it has received a good deal of emphasis and material support. There is some indication that U.S. policy-makers regard it as a possible prototype for other Latin American "sub-regional" security

---

[46]Central American countries have repeatedly been used as staging areas for operations against Cuba. For an account of the most famous such incident, see H. Johnson, The Bay of Pigs (New York: Dell Publishing Co., Inc., 1964).

arrangements or for a hemispheric inter-American defense force.[47]
The Central American experience, so far, suggests that external
support, while it may be conducive to the initiation of military
integration, is incapable of endowing it with any "naturally
expansive" propensities--much less of getting it to "spill over"
into adjoining policy areas. CONDECA is an example par excellence
of self-encapsulation.

Conclusion

Penetration by external political authorities and private
interests of the emerging Central American institutions and
processes has been extensive--perhaps more so than in any other
contemporary integration movement. And, as before, agents of a
single extra-regional power--the United States--continue to domi-
nate these efforts.[48] In the short run, this flow of external

---

[47]See the statements of President Johnson and Dean Rusk in the
New York Times, May 29 and May 30, 1965. In the words of Lt.
General R.H. Warren before a Congressional committee: "We have
encouraged this form of mutual cooperation [CONDECA] since we
believe that it can produce more security for less money" (U.S.
House of Representatives, Committee on Appropriations, Subcom-
mittee on Foreign Operations and Related Agencies, Foreign As-
sistance and Related Agencies Appropriations for 1971, Part I
[Washington, D.C.: Government Printing Office, 1970], p. 459).
For a comprehensive (and critical) assessment of CONDECA, see
John Saxe-Fernandez, "The Central American Defense Council and
Pax Americana" in Irving L. Horowitz, Josué de Castro, and John
Gerassi, eds., Latin American Radicalism (New York: Vintage
Books, 1969), pp. 75-101.

[48]Of course, the U.S. has not been alone in proffering external
support and guidance. ECLA played a key role during the formative
period, and has continued as an important source of technical
expertise, strategic thinking, ideological inspiration, elite
socialization, and alternative employment. Although its role
has gradually declined, ECLA's presence and willingness to serve
has made it a useful place to refer controversial items and new
issues for neutral, outside assessment and cooling off. The
U.N. itself has long provided assistance to regional bodies such
as ICAITI and ESAPAC/ICAP, and its specialized agencies are linked
to regional equivalents--e.g., ICAO and COCESNA, IMF and the
Central American Monetary Council. Several European countries
have pledged credits to CABEI; Venezuela and Colombia have explored participation in the Central American Monetary Council's
Clearing House. Mexico, however, has been the most active, of-
fering credit and technical assistance to national governments

resources has no doubt facilitated the implantation of the integration process. The induced investment has been associated with relative economic prosperity at the national level, however badly distributed its effects. The increased flow of loans and grants for multilateral or regional projects has not adversely affected bilateral flows to national governments and may even have stimulated them. In short, regionalism has set up an expanding-sum game wherein all apparently can gain simultaneously.[49] Also, the costs of maintaining regional organizations have been kept low for participants, and their contributions have had an obvious multiplier effect on the total resources available. To a degree, these have provided compensatory side-payments to member-states disadvantaged by the "natural" effects of unleashed and uncontrolled market forces. The self-proclaimed net losers in regional trade--Honduras and Nicaragua--have generally received more than "equal" shares of external support from CABEI, IADB, and AID sources since 1961-62 (see Table 4). The prospect of gaining access to such additional funds contributed much to the original integrative convergence (particularly in the case of Costa Rica's belated entry), and the subsequent prospect of losing them may have inhibited withdrawal (especially in the case of Honduras and Nicaragua).

Nevertheless, increased intrusion by public or private external actors has hardly been the unmitigated blessing some

---

and regional organizations. Despite Mexico's obvious interest in the area, it is still far from presenting an alternative to continued dependence on the United States.

[49]"In 1960, national and international development agencies together were contributing annually what amounted to $4 per capita to the countries of the Common Market. This represented at the time an average figure for such contributions in Latin America in general. Since then, aid to Central America has risen to between $6 and $7 per capita, considerably more than the present Latin American or global average" (Hansen, Central America, p. 45). Nota bene, however, the cautious and indirect language I have employed. Regional integration has "been associated" with prosperity, not "caused" it. What little research we have on Central American economic growth in the 1960-65 period indicates that most of it was due to unexpectedly good performance in the traditional export sector. Of the total average annual growth rate of 6.7 percent, only from 0.75 to a maximum of 1.2 percent can be linked directly or indirectly to the Mercomún. (See Donald H. McClelland, "The Common Market's Contributions to Central American Economic Growth: A First Approximation" in R. Hilton, ed., The Movement Toward Latin American Unity [New York: Praeger, 1969], pp. 508-536.)

Table 4

DISTRIBUTION OF EXTERNAL FUNDS BY COUNTRY IN CENTRAL
AMERICA: 1961/62-1968/69

	Honduras	Nicaragua	El Salvador	Guatemala	Costa Rica
Percent of CABEI Funds: 1962-68	24.1	22.9	19.3	19.0	14.7
Percent of IADB Funds: 1961-68	21.6	25.2	16.2	20.7	17.1
Percent of U.S. Economic Aid: 1962-69	18.0	29.6	20.0	11.5	21.1

Sources: B.O.L.S.A. Review, 3 (January 1969), p. 26; Inter-
American Development Bank, Activities 1961-1968; Agency
for International Development, Operations Report, w-
129 (Washington, D.C., 1969), pp. 44-45.

observers have claimed.[50]   Growing foreign control over domestic
industrial and financial institutions, declining tax revenues due
to the generous fiscal exemptions granted new external investment,
balances of payments made more difficult by debt repayment and
profit repatriation, rising consumer prices from protected,
foreign-owned assembly industries using little local manpower or
raw materials--all have begun to trigger a politicized reaction
to integration.   At the same time, the large-scale subsidization
of a dispersed set of regional organizations has left policy-
makers without a single authoritative center at the regional
level for responding to these new political challenges.[51]   Some

---

[50]See Cochrane, The Politics of Regional Integration, pp. 203-
218.   Even Wionczek finds "the attitude of United States . . .
coherent and largely positive" in his "Latin American Integration . . .," pp. 125-126.   For an enthusiastic endorsement of
the U.S. effort, bilateral and multilateral, see John F. McCamant,
Development Assistance in Central America (New York: Praeger,
1968).

[51]It is, of course, but a short step from making this observation to inferring that it is the outcome of a deliberate U.S.
policy of "divide and rule"--seeking to avoid the formation of
a single integrative center by encouraging institutional "spill-
around" and policy separability.   For some evidence of "doubts
that the supranational institutions of an integrated Latin America

institutions--for example, ODECA--have lost most of their regional
identity and are regarded as little more than subsidiaries of the
U.S. aid effort. Strong and overt U.S. initiatives in some policy
areas--e.g., educational planning through CSUCA, military unification through CONDECA, Panamanian entry through ODECA, promotion
of "free enterprise" through ROCAP subsidies to national and
regional entrepreneurial associations--have probably had counter-
productive results. Progress toward regional coordination in
these areas may be less likely than if the impetus had been more
indigenous. On the other hand, as Joseph Nye, Jr., has pointed
out, U.S. generosity may have "taught" regional actors that they
don't need to make equivalent financial sacrifices. In some
cases--e.g., ICAITI--national agencies and private firms have
grown accustomed to "free" or heavily subsidized services and
loans, and have proven reluctant to pay for these as the institutional workload increases or as external agency support is phased
out.

In general, then, the substantial and much-touted U.S.
aid to Central American economic integration, coupled with the
related success in attracting U.S. private investment, may have
diminished rather than increased the prospects for eventual Central American political integration. Granted that this pattern
of institutional "spill-around," as I have described it above,
might have emerged without the prompting of U.S. officials, and
granted that some of the issues around which politicization has
occurred might have developed with less as well as more external
penetration--nevertheless, more and more Central Americans have
begun to question the distribution of integrative benefits (within
and without the region), and few of them have much confidence in
the authenticity and/or authority of the region's embryonic political institutions for rectifying it. Policy externalization--i.e.,
the assertive elaboration and implementation of a joint stance
vis-à-vis external actors--could go a long way toward removing
many of these doubts, reestablishing the autochthonous image of
regional institutions, and, in the process, creating the sort of
dynamic and paramount political center to which national actors
might eventually transfer both their immediate expectations and
their ultimate loyalties. If this were the longer-term dialectical product of increased penetration, many might come to accept
it as a necessary--even a desirable--internal contradiction of
the integration process. Certainly, it is one peculiarly linked
to the region's future political configuration.

---

are [felt to be] in the interests of the U.S.," see Denham, pp.
213-216. See also Joseph Grunwald, "Latin American Economic
Development and the United States" in A.M. Piedra, ed., Socio-
Economic Change in Latin America (Washington, D.C.: Catholic
University Press, 1970), pp. 20-21.

Chapter 3

POLICY EXTERNALIZATION THROUGH REGIONAL ORGANIZATIONS

Policy Externalization

As previously noted, Central America began with a very
low level of policy externalization, and the five member-states
seemed reluctant to take on any new responsibilities in this
area. The General Treaty nowhere committed its signers to protracted, collective negotiations with outsiders. They did agree
"not to sign new unilateral treaties with non-Central American
countries affecting the principles of Central American economic
integration" and "to include the 'Central American Exception
Clause' in all trade agreements executed" (Article XXV). However,
no mention was made of a common trade policy,[52] and the Secretary-
General was not (as is customary in such treaties) specifically
empowered to represent the region before other governments or
international organizations.

Three provisions, however, implicitly invited externalization. The first was a reiteration of an earlier obligation
to establish a common external tariff within five years and to
ban all exemptions on third-party imports. This was bound to
stimulate reaction on the part of the area's trading partners
and to force upon members some awareness of the need for a self-
conscious regional trade policy. The second (to be found at
several points in the Treaty) empowered various bodies to seek
the support and advice of "other Central American and international organs." These (and corresponding clauses in the agreement
setting up CABEI) constituted an acknowledgment of the very considerable technical and intellectual assistance the movement had
been receiving from external sources, especially ECLA. They also
were hints of expectations of outside financial support, especially from the United States. The third provision inviting

---

[52]Interestingly, the short-lived Treaty of Economic Association
(1960) contained a more explicit mention of joint foreign policy-
making: "The Contracting Parties shall adopt a policy of cooperation and mutual consultation with regard to . . . their economic relations with countries outside Central America" (Article
VII). The watering-down of this provision in the General Treaty
immediately succeeding it suggests a deliberate "non-decision"
and member reluctance to externalize regional obligations.

externalization was the statement that the Treaty remained open
to the adhesion of any Central American state.

General Trade Policy

Despite the fragile legal base and the inauspiciously
low level of initial commitment, the ECLA evaluators of the first
five years of the integration process could already conclude that
"the concept of a national commercial policy toward the outside
world has practically lost all its significance." That no national representatives objected to such a blatant admission of lost
sovereignty is a sign of their awareness and acceptance of "a
de facto interdependence which transcends the scope of existing
integration treaties."[53] Whether or not they had been originally
aware of the implications (and I can find little in the written
record which indicates it), by agreeing to a regional determina-
tion of customs classification and levels of protection, they
were divesting themselves of unilateral control over one of the
principal instruments of foreign economic policy.

This de facto multilateralization was not, however, as
significant as it may first appear--if only because the Central
American countries had not been exercising their formal sovereign
rights and making concerted, aggressive use of trade policies.
Prior to the 1950's and 1960's, their essential concern, modified
somewhat by fiscal dependence upon custom revenues, was to facilitate cheap imports through low tariffs, most-favored-nation
clauses, and bilateral trade treaties with industrial countries.
Export trade was almost exclusively in the hands of foreign
producers, distributors, and creditors. Only subsequently, due
to the persistent imbalance between rising demands for foreign-
produced consumer and capital goods and stagnant demands for
domestically produced basic commodities, did the "radius of
action" of commercial policy expand, and national policy-makers
begin to experiment with trade and monetary policies designed to
adjust import levels to export earnings and foreign capital in-
flows and, concomitantly, to change import composition and promote
national industrial development.[54] Unlike the European experience, where the formation of a common commercial policy demands
the coordination of already operative and highly sophisticated
national policies, in Central America it involves creating a

---

[53]ECLA, Evaluación . . ., p. 14.

[54]See Charles A. Anderson, "Politics and Development Policy in
Central America," Midwest Journal of Political Science, V (November 1961), pp. 332-50.

policy de toutes pièces in the absence of previous experience or even organizational awareness.[55]

It is not clear, a priori, whether such a context of prior "non-decision-making" at the national level facilitates or inhibits the externalization of obligations. To a considerable extent, the answer may lie with the regional policies of external actors--with the schedule of incentives and dis-incentives advanced by extra-Central American powers, especially the United States. These environmental conditions, however, are not likely to be sufficient to explain the propensity for regional elites to respond collectively and actively. These elites may also be responding to opportunities and crises generated by their growing policy interdependence in "internal" matters. Regardless of the source of stimulus, the "fact" of interdependence and loss of unilateral control must be perceived by relevant elites and converted into strategies of influence and direction.

Economic administrators (técnicos) within the region have definitely seen this interdependencia de hecho and have sought to capitalize upon it. Their studies and proposals have grown increasingly insistent upon the need for more concerted and assertive regional action vis-à-vis third powers. Confronted from the start with a persistently negative balance on commercial account, and since 1965 by a marked instability in export earnings, national policy-makers seem to have learned the lesson with some conviction. They have, by and large, reacted positively to these SIECA-ECLA-UNCTAD messages, but have been decidedly restrained in responding to the requests for a partial transfer of foreign policy capacities to regional spokesmen which have accompanied these messages. Convinced of the need for a more assertive foreign economic policy, they have so far preferred to use regional organizations as sporadic and ad hoc instruments of national purpose to be chosen at their discretion--rather than to devolve such authority, regularly and irrevocably, upon these organizations.

The most obvious case of policy externalization is the acquisition and exercise by the new central organizations of the capacity for dealing in the name of the region as a whole with outsiders. SIECA and, to a lesser extent, the Executive and Economic Councils have repeatedly sought (despite the General Treaty's formal silence on the issue) institutional mandates to bargain in the name of Central America in a variety of international arenas.

First, within the regional context itself, representatives of SIECA, CABEI, ICAITI, ODECA, and the other regional secretariats

---

[55] See ECLA, Evaluación . . ., p. 75.

attend each others' meetings, where they participate actively--
presenting studies, introducing motions, accepting and passing
on new tasks, attempting to influence each others' policies, and,
in general, establishing a mutually satisfactory regional division
of labor.

Second, within the hemispheric and global contexts, these
representatives attend a wide variety of international confer-
ences--e.g., ECLA, IADB, OAS, IMF, UNCTAD, even the Preparatory
Commission for the Punta del Este summit meetings--where they
speak in the name of Central America. Although the regional organizations have not yet received formal and permanent diplomatic
representations, SIECA has maintained a permanent representative
in Europe since 1965 who is accredited to the EEC, and who par-
ticipated actively in the "Kennedy Round" GATT negotiations.[56]
On a less formal level of interaction, trade missions and roving
ambassadors have increasingly found a visit to SIECA, CABEI,
and/or ODECA a mandatory item in their itinerary. Usually well-
covered by the press and involving flattering references to the
region's "unprecedented success" in the field of integration,
these serve to enhance the prestige and legitimate the external
role of such regional organizations.

In two specific cases, the Common Market secretariat has
played a leading role in dealing with non-members. Panama had
initially declined to join either the political or the economic
integration movement. By the early 1960's it seemed to be
emerging from its isolationism, influenced perhaps by Costa
Rica's change of heart, the market's rapid commercial success,
and some prodding from the United States. In 1963, Panama's
President signed the "Declaration of Central America," announcing
his intention to seek an association with the Common Market
"through agreements that establish ties of economic cooperation."
Two years later, Panama's foreign minister made overtures to join
ODECA. While in the latter case, association has proved non-
controversial, and Panama began participating in ODECA's technical
councils, access to the more active and intensive set of economic
commitments has not advanced so smoothly. Central American entrepreneurs have expressed fear at the prospect of reexports of cheap
U.S. goods; monetary authorities seem reluctant to cooperate with
a country which has no national currency or Central Bank; Panamanian interest groups have been less than enthusiastic;[57] and

---

[56]Nicaragua is the region's only GATT member, and its representative is frequently used to present a coordinated position in
this forum. SIECA's European representative moved from Bruxelles
to Geneva to assist in such negotiations as the Kennedy Round.

[57]See Charles F. Denton, "Interest Groups in Panama and the
Central American Common Market," Inter-American Economic Affairs,
21 (1967), pp. 49-60.

the mercurial fortunes of Panamanian politicians during this period have made protracted discussion difficult. In this climate of uncertainty and controversiality, SIECA, charged with conducting the negotiations, has proceeded cautiously. It quietly farmed out the issue to a trio of private experts not associated with any of the regional public organizations. They filed their report, conditionally favorable to the eventual complete incorporation of Panama in mid-1967. However, the project ran into certain "areas of doubt" in the Economic Council. The subsequent emergence of other crises seems to have postponed the resolution of this external issue, but if it resumes, SIECA will presumably be called upon to play an important role.

The prospect of Central American incorporation into a wider, all-Latin American common market or free trade area has laid another external task upon the common market institutions. It has long been a tenet of ECLA integracionista ideology that Central America should consolidate its regional market as a prerequisite to later participation as a single unit in a continent-wide organization. To them, externalización--in the restricted sense of unit convergence with a more comprehensive system of interdependence--has always been considered one of the major goals of the integration movement. Although SIECA began studying the prospect in 1962, not until the hemispheric summit meeting of 1967 was some urgency injected. The assembled heads of state agreed to set up a joint LAFTA-CACM Commission. Instead, however, of placing primary responsibility on the respective secretariats, they specified that the actual negotiations are to be carried out by the Executive Council and, extraordinarily, by the Ministers of Economy themselves. The Central American Presidents not only agreed to eventually merge as a unit with Latin America, but reiterated their support for Panamanian incorporation and for discussions leading to "a rapid expansion of commercial and investment relations with neighboring countries and the Caribbean."[58] Some tentative "bloc" negotiations have already occurred with Mexico, Colombia, Venezuela, and the Dominican Republic. The area, then, of collective trade negotiations has been steadily expanding, as has the role of regional economic organization in them. Those who previously monopolized such inter-state, inter-institutional negotiations--the Ministers of Foreign Relations of the Five--have observed the trend with some misgiving. They have repeatedly demanded that they be kept informed and that they be consulted before a final collective agreement is drafted.

---

[58]SIECA, Carta Informativa, No. 67 (May 1967). The ECLA Evaluación report suggested using the forthcoming negotiations with Panama and Mexico as "trial runs" in policy externalization (p. 77).

Most of the externalization of mutual commitment which has occurred has not involved such formal, inter-institutional interaction. Rather, the Five have increasingly sought by ad hoc and sporadic means to coordinate their foreign economic policies.

The United Nations Conference on Trade and Development (UNCTAD) provided the first opportunity for formal interaction. Prior to the first conference in 1964, and again in 1967, the Ministers of Economy met "extraordinarily" and elaborated--on the basis of SIECA proposals--a common position. Although their demands later were subsumed into the joint Latin American position,[59] the Central Americans operated as a distinct "bloc" both at the hemispheric and global levels for the first time in international economic negotiations.

This precedent has been followed in numerous other international economic forums--so much so that prior joint consultation through the offices of common market institutions can probably be considered a definitive "acquisition," an expansion of scope, of the integration movement. Before the yearly meetings of ECLA, the Economic and Social Council of the OAS, and IADB, and before such occasional meetings as the International Consultative Committee on Cotton and the GATT negotiations, discussions are held. The joint position is usually expressed by one of the national representatives who, however, pointedly announces that he is speaking for the region as a whole. Secretariat representatives also attend these meetings, but are active primarily as consultants. In yet another field, the Five requested and received permission for the joint evaluation of their national development plans before an ad hoc committee of the Interamerican Council of the Alliance for Progress (CIAP).[60]

Nor have the planning, trade, and development officials been the only regional coordinators. The Central American monetary agreement, mentioned above, commits Central Bank officials

---

[59] Yet on one issue, the Central Americans broke with the Special Commission for Latin American Coordination (CECLA) and the larger UNCTAD "Group of 77." They pressed independently for special measures for smaller states. See Branislav Gosovic, "UNCTAD: North-South Encounter," International Conciliation, No. 568 (May 1968), p. 19.

[60] Report on Central American National Development Plans and the Process of Economic Integration (Washington, D.C.: Committee of Nine, Alliance for Progress, August 1966). The Report recommended that the SIECA-Joint Planning Commission be entrusted with coordinating all external assistance to the region (p. 28). Nothing became of this "expansive" suggestion.

to consultation on exchange policies. One of their first formal external actions was to ratify a credit and payments arrangement with Mexico. There is also some evidence of greater collaboration vis-à-vis international monetary institutions and foreign private banks. The Ministers of Labor and Social Security at their first meeting in 1964 agreed to coordinate activities in the International Labour Organization and various hemispheric bodies. Even the Directors of Civil Aviation have begun to send a single representative to International Civil Aviation Organization (ICAO) meetings and to split the costs.

These encouraging beginnings, however, should not lead one to assume that the Central American countries have definitively acquired a joint capacity for external action in these arenas. There is no unified Central American trade or economic policy as yet. One reason, as SIECA has repeatedly pointed out, is that individual countries still lack a coordinated national trade policy and institutions to back it up. Efforts to encourage them to create national foreign trade commissions and to cap these off with an all-Central American commission have failed so far.[61] SIECA has also stressed that the inflexible manner in which the level of external tariff protection is negotiated greatly limits the potentialities for "bloc" negotiations. It has sought (so far unsuccessfully) to use this dissatisfaction to increase the authority of regional entities by permitting the levels to be adjusted within certain margins without recourse to congressional ratifications.

---

[61]SIECA, Carta Informativa, No. 42 (April 1965). This same year SIECA created a special Commercial Policy Section.

Chapter 4

REGIONAL EFFORTS AT REGULATING FOREIGN CAPITAL
AND COMMODITY EXPORTS

In the preceding chapter, several fairly clear instances
of intersectional linkage at work are discussed. As the result
of policy performance in the original, "preferred" areas, interdependencies were activated and regional organizations expanded
the scope and the de facto authority of their activities to deal
with outside actors. For the most part, this expansion was
"cultivated" deliberately by national and regional administrators
who, forecasting on the basis of the ECLA doctrine, orthodox
economic theory, or the practice of other common market arrangements, anticipated emerging conflicts and acted before the directly affected interests could mobilize or even feel the pinch. In
one external area, however, they have had the issue thrust upon
them by protesting groups: the regulation of foreign capital.

As noted above, the visible success in attracting external
capital began to provoke a politicized reaction--by intellectuals,
some party leaders, and most of all, adversely affected domestic
industrialists. This came to a head in 1965 when the Federation
of Central American Chambers and Associations of Industry
(FECAICA) presented a manifesto to the assembled Ministers of
Economy.[62]

In the original convergence, no formal commitment was
made regarding limiting or guiding foreign investment. On the
contrary, it was recognized that trade liberalization and a more
protectionist common external tariff would stimulate such flows
and that each country would scramble to offer more attractive
fiscal exemptions for outside investors. The General Treaty did,
however, contain a clause obligating the signers to harmonize
their policies regarding such incentives (Article XIX).

The subsequent trajectory of this commitment to policy
harmonization well illustrates the political fragility of externalization processes. Initial agreement on uniform fiscal incentives was reached rather rapidly, and a formal protocol was

---

[62]See "Proyecto modificado del pronunciamiento de la FECAICA
en relación a las inversiones extranjeras en el área centroamericana," Guatemala, C.A., 26 March 1965; mimeo.

41

signed by all five countries in July 1962. Legislative ratifications were completed at the usual erratic pace; however, by
February 1965 all but Honduras had deposited them. SIECA-drafted
operative by-laws were advancing uneventfully through the Executive Council. It appeared that a successful externalization had
been accomplished--one which might provide the consensual basis
for future joint policies regulating foreign capital more broadly.

However, Honduras began raising objections--in effect, by
asserting the primacy of national policy outcomes over regional
(i.e., external) ones. While not opposed as such to a binding
joint agreement on fiscal incentives, its policy-makers argued
that a **uniform** policy would exacerbate a trend "uncovered" (they
asserted) by the first five years of operation of the General
Treaty: increasing inequity in the rate of return from regional
trade. With its initially lower level of development, Honduras
argued that it could not be expected to attract equal amounts of
foreign capital with equal incentives. When this prospect was
combined with the country's growing regional trade imbalance and
deteriorating terms of trade, the Honduran case became difficult
to dismiss.

In the Executive Council, called into extraordinary
session in January 1966, Honduras insisted on a special preferential protocol and refused to deposit the previously signed general
agreement. When the others failed to respond satisfactorily,
Honduras expanded its non-cooperation to a boycott on all out-
standing agreements and refused to attend any council meetings.
Meanwhile, Nicaragua began making similar noises about "unbalanced
returns," and the other members, faced with serious declines in
governmental revenue, began having second thoughts about having
granted such generous fiscal exemptions to foreign investors.
SIECA managed, after some six months of institutional paralysis,
to get out of the imbroglio by compartmentalizing the issues.
Salvadorean and Guatemalan counter-proposals and Costa Rican
"second thoughts" on the issue were shelved; Nicaragua's claim
was sent off for further study by ECLA (from which it has yet to
emerge); and Honduras' objections were dealt with in a special
protocol granting it a 20 percent marginal advantage. Even then,
"most deposits were made only under great political pressures."
Both the general and special incentive agreements became legally
effective in March 1969. Ironically, this hard-fought, partial
success at externalization never became operational, being swept
aside first by serious fiscal problems in several member countries
and then by the general collapse of Mercomún arrangements in the
aftermath of the Salvadorean-Honduran war.[63]

---

[63]This discussion of the attempt to meet the common fiscal incentives commitment and of Honduras' objection to it is based on
the extensive analysis of this crisis in Stuart Fagan's *Central*

Such attempts at "harmonization of incentives" have not met the principal objections of local entrepreneurs.[64] They have insisted repreatedly on the need to assign a "complementary" role to foreign capital--i.e., to restrict or ban it from "determined activities," to "orient" it toward non-competitive "new" fields, to ensure joint participation with indigenous capital and talent, to avoid the extension of incentives not available to nationals, and to guarantee priority on the part of national and regional financial institutions to the area's investors. All this, they have suggested, should be accomplished by means of a new Central American treaty. SIECA, the Executive Council, the Economic Council, the Central American Monetary Council, ODECA, and numerous ad hoc meetings of officials have all gone on record agreeing that such an "orientation" is both desirable and necessary,[65] yet nothing has been done. No new mutual obligation has been accepted.

The ECLA Evaluación report noted, optimistically, that no disagreement existed as to what should be done or how it could be done, but "difficulties have arisen in reaching a similar consensus on the operative aspects of the policy." In short, each country is afraid that such an agreement would either scare off foreign investment altogether or benefit the others disproportionately. Also, such a regional agreement would have to be sufficiently "flexible" to permit decisions to be made collectively on the merits of each case--which entails the sort of spill-

---

American Economic Integration: The Politics of Unequal Benefits (Berkeley: Institute of International Studies, University of California, 1970), pp. 23-36. [Research Series, No. 15]

[64]On the contrary, as Miguel Wionczek has pointed out, the new regional Convenio was more generous with fiscal exemptions and tariff privileges and lacking in controls than the previous national laws ("La integración económica latinoamericana y la inversión privada extranjera," Comercio Exterior, XX [September 1970], p. 755). Strong pressures have already been exerted for its revision.

[65]See JOPLAN, "Centroamérica: Lineamientos para una política de desarrollo regional" (Guatemala, C.A., September 1964), mimeo; CABEI, "Bases para la formulación de una política regional en materia de fomento de inversiones" (Tegucigalpa, March 1965), mimeo; SIECA, "Nota de Secretaría sobre inversiones extranjeras" (Guatemala, C.A., June 1965), mimeo. Carlos Castillo, in his recent speech of resignation as Secretary-General of SIECA, made a strong plea for the "orientation" of foreign capital (see SIECA, Carta Informativa, No. 106 [August 1970]). Nevertheless, none of the subsequent drafts aimed at a new modus operandi contained a commitment to this end.

over in the level of authoritative regional decision-making which the members have so far been reluctant to grant.

The regional técnicos have approached the issue in their usual cautious, circuitous "pragmatic" style. They have placed the issue under protracted (but unhurried) study. They are also trying to creep up on it incrementally--through clauses in the Integration Industries and Special System protocols,[66] by restrictions in textile agreements, by promoting certain uniform standards of project evaluation in the countries, by influencing the lending policies of CABEI, by resolutions of the Monetary Council concerning the purchase of private banks, and by suggesting the possible harmonization of laws regarding forest and subsoil rights and those governing joint ventures of all types. These partial, selective measures (most of which have not yet borne fruit) permit the accumulation of a set of less visible regional obligations which would circumscribe ("orient" is the preferred term) the role of foreign capital while avoiding the sort of open conflict which would underscore the divergence of member policies and frighten off the foreign entrepreneur, so notoriously sensitive to the "investment climate."[67]

Meanwhile, Central America remains an uncontrolled "happy hunting ground" for external capital, and the magnitude of the contradiction between the Common Market's stimulus to the activity of aggressive foreign investors and the nationalistic sensitivities of threatened domestic entepreneurs increases. The regional técnicos may, in the future, be able to capitalize on this and emerge as the patriotic defenders of Central American industrialists against foreign capitalists and their domestic political allies. The eventuality of such a shifting alliance would be facilitated by prior incremental successes at intergovernmental harmonization and by the expanding role of the Integration Bank as a channelizer of investment funds, projects, and expertise.

This, of course, is pure conjecture. So far the "orientation" of the foreign capital issue merely illustrates particularly well the emergence of pressures for an external spill-over and the pragmatic strategy of regional decision-makers, which has sought to promote modest expansions in the scope of mutual

---

[66]For example, clauses in the three "integration industry" agreements oblige the firms to offer varying proportions of common stock to Central American investors. See David E. Ramsett, Regional Industrial Development in Central America (New York: Praeger, 1969).

[67]For an outline (implicit) of this gradualist strategy, see ECLA, Evaluación . . . , pp. 57-59.

commitment, but has avoided or postponed overt moves aimed at increasing the level of regional authority.[68]

Commodity Export Policy

As the propensity to externalize regional obligations gathers momentum and begins to involve new policy sectors, Central Americans have quickly had to face the reality, not only of the preponderant importance of trade with extra-regional economies, but especially of the major role which basic agricultural commodities continue to play in that trade. With coffee, cotton, and bananas accounting for approximately 75 percent of the total exports from the area, it is difficult to imagine how effective and consequential coordination of regional policy vis-à-vis the outside world could avoid these traditional sectors.[69]

The policy sectors over which regional organizations have so far extended their control are relatively "unpopulated" or "unattended" by policy-making institutions. This is hardly the case with respect to Central America's most important export: coffee. In the three countries where coffee is the dominant commodity--Costa Rica, Guatemala, and El Salvador--its exportation

---

[68]An excellent example of what a "successful" policy externalization in this sector might look like (and the problems it is likely to raise) is being provided by the new foreign investment code of the Andean Bloc. In this case, Colombia, Chile, Peru, Bolivia, and Ecuador have agreed, at the initiation of their integration process, on a very comprehensive set of norms restricting external capital to specified sectors, enforcing local participation (as well as the eventual self-liquidation of foreign control of enterprises), controlling rates of profit remittance and capital reinvestment, and limiting access to internal capital sources. Although there are gaping loopholes, and enforcement is left in the hands of national commissions, this is an unprecedented step, perhaps in part the result of "negative learning" from Central America's unfortunate experience. (For the text of the Treaty, see Comercio Exterior [February 1971], pp. 114-122.) These efforts at policy externalization have been sharply opposed by U.S. private sector groups, although the U.S. government has remained silent on the issue. See Miguel S. Wionczek, "La reacción norteamericana ante el trato común a los capitales extranjeros en el Grupo Andino," Comercio Exterior (May 1971), pp. 406-408.

[69]The General Treaty (Article IV) specifically excludes intrazonal exchanges in these traditional commodities from trade liberalization in Appendix A to the Treaty.

is well protected by an interlocking set of public and private
oficinas, institutos, asociaciones, and compañías. These "autar-
chic" agencies operate, as their titles imply, quite independently
of ministerial or even Central Bank control.

These "privatized" agencies have had very little prior
regional cooperative experience. Producing the same type coffee
("milds") and maintaining separate and intimate contacts with
distributors and consumers, they have long regarded each other
primarily as competitors. They were all members of the Federación
Cafetalera de América (FEDECAME), but this group included all
Latin American producers except Brazil and Colombia (14 in all).
FEDECAME played only a modest role in international coffee negotiations. Its heterogeneous composition prevented its taking a
more vigorous stand, and it was not successful in forging special
links between its Central American members.

An excellent example of the absence of regional trust and
consciousness among coffee producers occurred in 1964, years
after cooperation was well advanced in other arenas. Costa Rica,
as a result of volcanic activity, experienced a dramatic shortfall
in production and was unable to fill its international quota.
Its neighbors requested Costa Rican support for an International
Coffee Agreement (ICA) resolution giving them preference in sup-
plying the deficit. Costa Rica adamantly refused.[70]

The operation of the ICA (negotiated in 1963) has had a
paradoxical impact upon the efforts by the Central Americans to
coordinate their coffee policies. On the one hand, its initial
impact was to stabilize prices at a more profitable level. This
tended to reduce the incentive for a joint response--especially
when one introduces the institutional factor that, if the Central
Americans were to seek a single regional quota, they would lose
votes in the ICA. On the other hand, the higher prices stimulated
production to such an extent that all are now suffering from
surplus and stocking problems. Previously, Costa Rica's more
"balanced" production had impeded its participation; now they
are all in the same boat. Add to this a subsequent decline in
prices (especially in "milds") and a tightening up on ICA controls
over dumping and such subterfuges as "cafés turistas," and the
result is an impressive sum of external pressures for a regional
convergence.

---

[70]I was confidentially informed that there has been a substantial amount of illicit coffee trade between the "Northern Three"
(Guatemala, Honduras, and El Salvador), designed to fill shortfalls and/or to avoid quota restrictions altogether. This, however, has been a strictly private (and illegal) venture, not
convincing evidence of regional policy coordination.

It has, however, been slow in coming. In 1966, for example, the Central Americans were faced with an imminent 2 1/2 percent cut in their quotas because of declining prices. Only strong outside pressures from Brazil and Colombia (who feared an individualist dumping reaction which might have affected prices of other types of coffee)[71] forced them to band together temporarily. The Economist observed that, since the sale of "milds" has usually been bunched into a few months,

> it has long been realized that the Central Americans would do better to spread their sales over the year [but] . . . none [of them] have trusted each other enough to work such a scheme. Brazil's contribution to the rescue operation two months ago was conditional on the three big Central American producers coming together to coordinate their sales. Two months later, however, the $1.8 million pooled . . . has been spent and [they] are no nearer coordinating their sales. They now look like having to pay the stiff penalty for failing to cooperate.[72]

Prior to the ICA Conference of 1967, they did begin to move coordinately. The Central Americans, with Mexico, met several times and elaborated their own five-point position. Although they avoided such substantive issues as coordination of sales, and left each country to bargain individually for quota increases, a start was made toward a distinctive Central American stance. In 1968, the Five finally formed a permanent association: the Central American Coffee Organization.

In interviews with the author during the summer of 1967, coffee officials--public and private--expressed doubt about the desirability of a joint regional quota, and were opposed to merging their respective agencies into a single Central American Coffee Institute--even though many pointed out proudly that this would make them the world's third largest coffee producer. All, however, expressed interest in the establishment of more regular and frequent forms of regional cooperation, but denied rather vehemently that the institutions of the Common Market had anything to do with their recent convergence.

Not that the CACM institutions have not discussed the issue. Meetings at a variety of levels (técnico, ministerial,

---

[71]Indeed, several months later (February 1967), El Salvador did just that--acted on its own and dumped 250,000 bags at four cents under the floor price, effecting a three-cent drop in other types. See Hansen, Central America, p. 8.

[72]The Economist, December 24, 1966, pp. 1347-8.

inter-ministerial, even presidential) and in a variety of forums
(ad hoc meetings, Committee on Economic Cooperation, SIECA, Executive Council, Economic Council, ODECA) have produced suggestions
concerning a possible coffee policy and even the creation of a
Central American Coffee Commission.[73] Nothing has resulted
directly from these discussions. The recent successful resistance
on the part of coffee growers to the initiation of diversification
programs and to the implementation of tax reforms is impressive
evidence of the political impregnability of this sector. Even
with strong executive support at the national level, it is doubtful that "outsiders" can force a spill-over into regional coffee
policy. Only some configuration of external incentives and market
crisis--both beyond the control of regional authorities--seems
likely to generate a lasting convergence in this encapsulated,
privatized sector of the economy.

Cotton, the area's second largest export crop, may prove
less resistant. It is both newer (large-scale exports date from
the late 1950's), and more dynamic (average increases in exports
of 35 percent annually from 1960 to 1964). However, cotton market
prices have been highly volatile.

Central American cotton production is also concentrated
in three countries: Nicaragua, El Salvador, and Guatemala; however, only in the former is it the predominant earner of foreign
exchange. It would seem that regional cotton growers are less
likely than coffee producers to be so institutionally entrenched
within their respective national polities. They carry less
weight, have less experience, sell more of their product to
domestic consumers, and are more dependent upon governmental
support for technical assistance, fertilizers, pesticides, etc.
Add to this the relative stagnation in the world demand for cotton, increasing competition from synthetics, growing world surplus production (since 1961), and greater aggressiveness on the
part of the United States in export markets (since 1965), and
one finds an exceedingly vulnerable economic sector.[74]

Predictably, regional cotton producers have moved more
rapidly toward policy coordination than have coffee growers. In
March 1966, at the initiative of Guatemala, the Central American

---

[73]ECLA, Evaluación . . . , pp. 141-2.

[74]This brief summary is based upon the treatment in Hansen,
Central America, pp. 8-9. The U.S. decision in 1965 to export
cotton stocks has had a direct impact on Central American sales.
Hansen reports that some countries experienced declines in total
value of cotton exports and that several are suffering from
rising production costs.

Front of Cotton Producers was established. They began immediately
to exchange information on marketing and production, and to establish a common grading system and quality controls, and agreed to
support jointly a Regional Institute of Cotton Research in San
Salvador. Regional prices on cottonseed were established under
their aegis; by 1969, they were fixing prices on cotton itself.[75]
The Front also began to place demands upon regional authorities.
It complained before the Executive Council of tariff preferences
being granted to animal oils for the manufacture of cooking oil
and margarine, and obtained a favorable ruling. It expressed its
support for a comprehensive regional textile agreement. More
important, it raised, for the first time, the issue of the impact
of higher-cost, regionally produced industrial goods upon the
production costs of domestic exports. A Costa Rican fertilizer
plant had demanded an upward renegotiation of protective tariffs,
and the cotton producers vigorously, collectively, and successfully opposed it. Despite the possible implications of such
resistance for their desired goal of import substitution, the
regional técnicos have regarded this autonomous form of regional
external collaboration with approval.[76] When the Front took a
joint stand to the XXVIth Session of the International Consultative Committee on Cotton in Amsterdam in 1967, SIECA's European
representative also attended and backed them up with a special
report.

In cotton, then, a different pattern of externalization
has emerged. Initially triggered by extra-regional pressures and
articulated quite independently, this new private regional organization was subsequently (and very quickly) forced to interact
with, and appeal to, regional public agencies. This relationship
has been reinforced by the need for technical expertise to bargain
at the global institutional level. Hence, despite their antagonism to some of the basic objectives of the Common Market, especially in manufactured goods, the cotton growers of the area
became part of the emerging network of interdependence underlying
the integration process.

Bananas represent still another type of response. Although cotton is a new crop, its interests are already being
protected and promoted by the same sort of (admittedly less in-
fluential) mixed public-private institutos or consejos as coffee.

---

[75]See William Hunter, "Central American Producers Unite to Push
Cotton," Cotton International (1967), pp. 172ff.; B.O.L.S.A. Review, June 1969, p. 380, and November 1969, p. 700.

[76]See SIECA, Informe sobre los avances del programa de Integración Económica Centroamericana, Febrero de 1966, Mayo de 1967
(Guatemala, C.A., 1967: mimeo).

The transport, marketing, and, to a lesser extent, production of
bananas is almost completely beyond national control--in the hands
of a small number of North American firms. However, the Central
American countries no longer deserve the pejorative epithet
"banana republics." Plant diseases, political uncertainty, and
rising nationalism have resulted in a decline in both the production and the political fortunes of the United Fruit Company.[77]
Recent introduction of the disease-resistant Valery banana and
a redefinition of relationships between national authorities and
United Fruit have resulted in better production and export prospects. However, Central American governments have yet to establish their control over external policy in this sector.

Under these inauspicious circumstances--of relatively
favorable market perspectives and unfavorable political prece-
dents--it is perhaps surprising that any moves toward regional
policy coordination should have been made. Vague initiatives
by SIECA and ODECA aiming at either pressuring the foreign companies into setting aside a portion of their revenues for regionally oriented research and promotion or establishing a Banana
Institute have produced no results. The prospect of greater
import restrictions by EEC on bananas from non-associated states,
however, brought about a rapid convergence. The Executive and
Economic Councils joined company officials in forming a "United
Central American Front" opposing the impending EEC measures,
establishing a joint position at forthcoming CIAP and FAO meetings
on the subject, and rejecting collectively the drafting of an
international convention restricting banana production. Several
months later a "high level mission" coordinated by ODECA and
SIECA was assembled to press the issue directly before the European institutions. The resolution creating the mission came from
the Foreign Ministers' Conference of December 1967, and included
the "expansive" recommendation that member governments take advantage of this opportunity to adopt permanent measures for jointly responding to such "discriminatory" threats in the future.
Were this to become effective, the Central American countries
would be taking a considerable, even transcendental, step toward
institutionalized externalization. In all likelihood, such an
expansion in scope would have to be accompanied by some devolution
of authority to a regional center.

Sugar and meat are Central American exports of minor, but
increasing, importance. Like coffee and cotton, their domestic

---

[77]Bananas currently account for approximately 15 percent of
total area exports. See Stacy May and Galo Plaza, The United
Fruit Company in Latin America (Washington, D.C.: National
Planning Association, 1958) for an analysis of the declining
fortunes of the industry.

fortunes are protected by small, politically well-connected elites organized around self-governing, semi-public corporatist groups and agencies. Their external prospects lie, however, exclusively in the hands of U.S. policy-makers, since virtually all exports are to the United States and are subject to its direct controls. Hence, externalization consists of lobbying--individually or collectively--before governmental agencies and the U.S. Congress.

Formerly, the lobbying over the sugar quota was an extremely individualistic and, if one is to believe the anecdotal literature, ruthlessly competitive enterprise. Since the foundation of the Central American Federation of Sugar Producers in 1960-61, the Five have joined forces. They have repeatedly acted as a unit through their front organization in Washington (The Central American Sugar Council) and collective diplomatic representations (usually led by the doyen of the diplomatic corps, the Nicaraguan ambassador). The U.S. Sugar Act prohibits reexports, but in 1965--as the result of bloc pressures--an amendment granted other Central American producers priority in filling shortfalls from the area. U.S. authorities decide on the distribution, but their handling of this situation is an important example of external responsiveness to the emerging regional community.[78]

Such lobbying vis-à-vis the United States was not the prime or original motive for creating the Federation, however. Although, like the other major traditional export commodities, sugar was excluded from the liberalization provisions of the General Treaty, it has been an important item in intra-regional trade, due to large differences in internal prices and vagaries in production. According to interview sources, the original convergence was motivated by a desire to exchange information on "threatening" government policies--i.e., tax and land reform-- and to control the trade which might develop as a result of general liberalization.[79] The U.S. prohibition on reexports and upon granting quotas to countries which themselves are importing from others helped to legitimate this cartelization scheme.

---

[78]In several successive decisions, Central American producers have seen their quotas modestly increased. Brazil and the Dominican Republic have consistently received the most favored treatment, however. See B.O.L.S.A. Review, July 1969, p. 449, and September 1969, p. 584.

[79]In the words of one respondent: "Why should we undermine each other's prices? We are all Central Americans, aren't we?"-- a reminder that regional consciousness can diminish as well as increase transactions.

The ranchers and meatpackers of Central America have recently begun an analogous process of externalization at the regional level. Their rising exports were dependent upon quotas set by the U.S. Meat Import Act. As early as 1965, SIECA had called a meeting of cattle experts and exporters and had accepted several advisory tasks, including serving as intermediary with the United States for possible regional preferential treatment.[80] Two years later, faced with a threatened unilateral cut in their quotas due to pressures by U.S. ranchers, the Central Americans banded together for the first time in a federation. As the inevitable first step, they opened a lobby in Washington. (I was told they began by using the services of the regional sugar lobbyist.) Their efforts do not yet seem to have had the same restrictive impact on intra-regional trade as those of the sugar producers; live cattle remains a fairly important item in intra-regional commerce.

Of all the traditional export sectors, cotton and sugar demonstrate most clearly the indirect consequences of regional trade liberalization upon cooperation in external policy. Coffee is still too competitive, too nationally impregnable; bananas escape regional or national control; meat is of too little significance. The cotton and sugar interest representatives interviewed admitted readily that their new efforts at collaboration had been influenced either by the example of the Common Market (learning effects) or by issues which arose indirectly from trade liberalization (engrenage effects). Representatives from the other three sectors insisted that extra-regional market conditions exclusively had stimulated their collective responses. All insisted that public regional organizations had had no direct influence over their activities.

The examples of cotton and sugar illustrate well, however, that indirectly stimulated, independent externalization can have differing consequences for the integration process as a whole. In the case of cotton, it has led to increasing interaction and exchanges of demands and supports. It could eventually result in an incorporation and permanent extension of scope, coordinated from the center. In the case of sugar, the response has been defensive and negative, leading to a decline in regional trade and to no organizational interaction with the new regional authorities. It constitutes a near perfect case of sectoral self-encapsulation at the regional level.

The response of regional authorities to these independent, semi-public efforts at externalization has been cautious. Despite

---

[80]SIECA, _Carta Informativa_, No. 48 (October 1965). SIECA suggestions aimed at coordinating purchasing and marketing in order to open European markets have not succeeded.

frequent resolutions and pronouncements on the desirability of a governmental regional export policy, the técnicos and ministers have generally expressed support for these private ventures and have avoided any confrontations, either by creating competing public institutions or by appealing over their heads to higher national authorities. SIECA created within itself an External Trade Policy Section which has studied several of these traditional export issues. It also has been quietly urging greater cooperation between Ministers of Economy and of Foreign Relations in the coordination of a Central American position at international trade conferences, commodity agreements, and other "bloc" negotiations.[81]

In the absence of such a high level convergence (which might bring some of the autonomous commodity institutes into line), SIECA has opted for a characteristically indirect strategy. With the help of ECLA, CABEI, and some ROCAP funds, it has placed a major emphasis on the discovery and promotion of new exports. A regional Center for the Promotion of Exports will eventually be created, and governments are being encouraged to establish national counterparts. Hopefully this, plus its activity in running Central American exhibits at international fairs, will permit the Secretariat to acquire, gradually and with low salience, a reputation for competence in external trade matters and some institutional strength at the national level which it can later use to assert control over the vastly more important and controversial areas of traditional exports. Of course, to the degree that its efforts at trade diversification are successful, the ultimate attempt at policy consolidation will be correspondingly easier.

---

[81]The Ministers of Foreign Relations in ODECA have often expressed an interest in such a joint ministerial venture. See, for example, the resolutions of the Second Conference, November 1966 in San José, Boletín Informativo de la ODECA (November-December 1966), pp. 8-9. This issue was placed before the Ministers of Economy in the Economic Council session of August 1967. SIECA urged some permanent institutional collaboration; the Economic Ministers were reluctant to share the responsibility and agreed only to sporadic, ad hoc joint discussions (SIECA, Carta Informativa, No. 71 [September 1967]).

Chapter 5

FOREIGN POLICY AND REGIONAL COHESION

One might anticipate that, eventually, regional actors charged with general responsibility for the conduct of foreign affairs would become affected by specialized "sectoral" efforts at regional policy externalization. If not as the result of engrenage or integrative learning, foreign ministers and their representatives at the least are likely to suffer from "fallout"-- a potential decline in status as other ministerial actors acquire additional prestige, influence, and resources from their success- ful participation in regional organizations. They are likely to respond by trying to "get in on the act" at the regional level (hence, the revived interest in the Organization of Central American States [ODECA] in the mid-1960's) and/or at the extra- regional level by harmonizing policy goals vis-à-vis individual countries and within international organizations.

Determining whether a general foreign policy harmonization has occurred among the Central American countries and, if so, how it is related to the economic integration process is no easy task: first, because it is difficult to establish whether the units have any distinctive foreign policies of their own, and second, because in terms of their voting performance in international or- ganizations, their positions were substantially convergent before the economic integration movement began.

The paramount foreign policy objective of most Central American countries has traditionally been to ensure, by all means possible, the presence of "compatible" regimes in neighboring states. Personal enmities, differing levels of internal stability and legitimacy, continuous plotting by embittered exiles, ill- defined and ill-guarded frontiers--all have more or less guaran- teed that subversion, assassination, armed invasion, vitriolic propaganda, and bribery would be the "currencies" of foreign policy within the region. Alliances would be shifting, oppor- tunistically engaged in, and rapidly dissolved, leaving lasting scars but few patterns of stable collaboration--hardly a propi- tious climate for policy harmonization.

By the 1960's, the number and intensity of "hostile inci- dents" seemed to be declining.[82] But this apparent long-term

---

[82]See Joseph S. Nye's cautious conclusion: "In Central America

trend could not be visibly linked to joint and permanent organizational efforts in either the political (ODECA) or the economic
(CACM) realms. The increased effectiveness of the OAS in collective security matters, the unchallenged hegemony of the United
States, and the gradual resolution of several border disputes
contributed to the establishment of an apparent "security community"--i.e., "long time dependable expectations of 'peaceful
change' among [the] population."[83] A new "cooperation" was en-
gendered by the abortive revolution in Guatemala (1954) and the
successful one in Cuba (1958/9). Fear that populist, militant
nationalist, or Communist elements might profit from border
squabbles, invasions by exiles, or even vitriolic personal disputes between heads-of-state encouraged the emergence of a new
"norm of reciprocity." The creation of CONDECA and the regular
exchange of information about each other's "subversives" seemed
to institutionalize the political status quo and guarantee mutual
toleration by differing regimes. Even such historic enemies as
Nicaragua's Anastasio Somoza and Costa Rica's José Figueres seemed
to have "buried the hatchet,"[84] and no national military seemed
to be plotting the invasion of any other Central American country.[85] These developments (later to prove so fragile in the case

---

. . . there has been a general decline of hostile incidents between the five states from the 1950's to the early 1960's. . . .
It is also interesting, though only partially causally significant, that the number of incidents is inversely related to the
growth of economic integration. . . ." ("Comparative Regional
Integration: Concept and Measurement," International Organization, XXII [Autumn 1968], p. 873 [emphasis added]).

[83]Karl Deutsch et al., Political Community in the North Atlantic
Area (Princeton: Princeton University Press, 1957), p. 2. The
best treatment of this subject in the "Pan-American" context is
Jerome Slater, The OAS and United States Foreign Policy (Columbus,
Ohio: Ohio State University Press, 1967), pp. 63-134.

[84]See John Martz, Central America (Chapel Hill: University of
North Carolina Press, 1959), pp. 185-92. Support from "friendly"
neighboring countries continued to be a part of national politics.
For example, an overflight of Nicaraguan jets at a crucial moment
in 1963 helped bolster the sagging fortunes of the Ydígoras
Fuentes regime in Guatemala. Later that same year, a similar
show of support contributed to the success of a golpe in Honduras.
Afterwards, the new dictator, López Arellano, paraded through the
streets of Tegucigalpa in Somoza's own bulletproof limousine.

[85]In retrospect, it is clear that more importance should have
been assigned to the sporadic acts of hostility on the El Salvadorean-Honduran border. On one occasion in 1967, for example,

of El Salvador and Honduras) left the foreign ministers of the area free to collaborate in other extra-regional contexts.

The U.S. "presence" in Central America--its physical proximity, multiple assymetric linkages, and declared security interests in the region--would seem to ensure that these five countries would behave similarly in such forums as the United Nations, and that their performances would be identical to or at least compatible with that of the United States. In this context, "intra-Central American agreement" would be completely spurious-- causally unrelated to collaborative efforts in other sectors.

None of the by now numerous studies of voting patterns in the United Nations mentions the existence of a distinctive Central American bloc.[86] A discernible Latin American group, with which the Five have usually been classified, does exist, both as a regularly convened caucus[87] and as a cluster of voting

---

the President of El Salvador, General Sánchez Hernández, covertly supported a garrison uprising against the reigning dictator of Honduras, General López Arellano, and was caught in the act. (See Vincent Cable, "The 'Football War' and the Central American Common Market," International Affairs, 43 [October 1969], p. 661.)

[86]Thomas Hovet, Jr., Bloc Politics in the United Nations (Cambridge: Harvard University Press, 1960); M. Margaret Ball, "Bloc Voting in the General Assembly," International Organization, V (February 1951), pp. 3-31; F.H. Seward, "The Changing Balance of Power in the United Nations," The Political Quarterly, 28 (October-December 1957), pp. 316-327; Robert Riggs, Politics in the United Nations (Urbana: University of Illinois Press, 1958); Geoffrey Goodwin, "The Expanding United Nations, I--Voting Patterns," International Affairs, 36 (April 1960); Arend Lijphart, "The Analysis of Bloc Voting in the General Assembly: A Critique and Proposal," American Political Science Review, LVII (December 1963), pp. 902-917; Bruce Russett, International Regions and the International System (Chicago: Rand McNally, 1967), pp. 59-93. For Latin America in particular, see John S. Houston, Latin America in the United Nations (New York: Carnegie Endowment, 1956).

[87]According to Houston, the group began to meet informally as early as the first General Assembly in London, initially for the purpose of electing Latin Americans to key positions. Since then, its activities have been extended to cover substantive issues (ibid., pp. 6-7). Ricardo Alfaro, a Panamanian active in the Latin American caucus, has observed that "the result of these meetings more often than not is only to bring forward the different criteria existing among the several governments" (ibid., "Introduction"). Riggs arrives at a similar conclusion (p. 23).

similarities.[88] However, the studies of voting patterns are unanimous in their conclusion that it is one of the least cohesive of the U.N. blocs. We shall attempt to discover whether Central America forms a more cohesive "sub-bloc" or faction within the larger bloc, and whether its cohesion has increased since 1961/2.

If one examines all non-unanimous U.N. General Assembly roll call votes from 1946 to 1968 (total N = 2,978),[89] and calculates for the five-nation Central American subset an Index of Relative Cohesion,[90] there is evidence to support the contention that these countries have tended increasingly to concord in their international voting pattern. If one compares the pre-integration (1946-51) average score with the post-integration (1952-68) mean, he finds an increase from 32 percent to 58 percent greater cohesion than all U.N. members combined. If the time cut is made in 1962, when the General Treaty really began taking effect, the results are even more impressive. The 1946-61 mean was 60 percent; the mean for 1962-68 was 83 percent.

Of course the general voting pattern ranges over a wide variety of issues. Table 5 breaks the roll calls into three specific areas: economic, military-diplomatic, and human rights. While in all three areas there is evidence of increased concordance, surprisingly, in the area within which interaction and institutional growth was the greatest (economic) and during the period in which this reached its apex (1962-66), Central American voting cohesion lessened! Agreement in more political matters,

---

[88]See Russett, pp. 74 et seq., and Lijphart, p. 917.

[89]This longitudinal analysis of Central American voting in the United Nations is based on data compiled and made available by Edward T. Rowe. I am grateful to Ernst B. Haas for providing the cross-tabulations which appear in Tables 5-8.

[90]The Index of Relative Cohesion is calculated by comparing the cohesion scores for a subset of countries with the mean cohesion scores for the U.N. membership as a whole during the same period. It is computed as follows: Cohesion scores for pairs of countries are calculated according to the Index of Agreement proposed by Arend Lijphart (see footnote 86 above); the mean Index of Agreement among the pairs of countries is taken as the overall cohesion score of the subset; the mean Index of Cohesion for the entire U.N. membership is expressed as O; and the difference between O and the score of the subset is the group's "relative cohesion score"--the measure used in these tables. (The Index of Relative Cohesion was devised by Edward T. Rowe.)

Table 5

CENTRAL AMERICAN COHESION IN U.N. ROLL CALL VOTES: 1946-1968

(In percent)

Issues	1946-1951	1952-1956	1957-1961	1962-1966	1967-1968	Mean for 1952-1968	Gain/Loss in Cohesion
All (N = 2,978)	32%	45%	56%	77%	63%	58%	+26%
Economic (N = 212)	57	57	73	29	86	60	+3
Military-Diplomatic (N = 1,657)	29	35	48	76	65	52	+23
Human Rights (N = 742)	15	50	59	85	57	61	+46

where progress within the region was slight, showed a tendency to increase in the global forum![91]

This performance on economic issues challenges any simplistic assumptions about learning and inter-institutional transfer. While the percentage of agreement among the Five was 57 percent higher than the United Nations as a whole in 1946-51 and 1952-56, increasing to 73 percent in 1957-62, when the institutional foundations were being laid within the region, it plummeted to 29 percent in 1962-66, recovering to 86 percent in the final time period covered (1967-68).

Table 6 pinpoints this paradoxical finding. There the various economic issues are subclassified by substantive topic. The decline in cohesion in 1962-66 is shown to be due in large measure to differences in voting on "science and technology" issues and, to a lesser extent, on issues in a catchall category: "trade/development/science/technology." These are not topics which have been subjects of extensive debate and interaction at the regional level. "Technical assistance" and "U.N. capital development agencies" have, however, and there also one finds less cohesion in the 1962-66 period. On the other hand, voting on issues relating to the "world trading system" reflects very clearly a sustained high degree of regional consensus after the founding of Central American institutions.

So far, the longitudinal evidence suggests (but by no means proves) that the Central Americans are acting or, better, voting more cohesively in global international policy matters as an indirect consequence of regional processes. An alternative explanation is that there is nothing special about the Central American subset, but that the increased concordance is a more generally Latin American phenomenon, reflecting the influence of ECLA-generated intellectual currents. Table 7 permits us to test this theory, as well as to compare Latin American regional performance with those of other regional groupings.

In the overall rankings in post-integration cohesion across all issues, the Central Americans agreed 58 percent of the time--below the 63 percent of the LAFTA grouping but considerably above the 42 percent of the OAS. On specifically economic issues, however, the Five rank above LAFTA and the OAS, but below such "established" regional organizations as Comecon, the East African Common Market (EACM), the Nordic Council, and the Arab

---

[91]One should note that after monotonic increases in each successive time period since 1946, the Index of Relative Cohesion on both military-diplomatic and human rights issues decreased in the latest (1967-68) time period.

Table 6

CENTRAL AMERICAN COHESION IN U.N. ROLL CALL VOTES ON SPECIALIZED ECONOMIC ISSUES: 1946-1968

(In percent)

Issues	1946-1951	1952-1956	1957-1961	1962-1966	1967-1968	Mean for 1952-1968	Gain/Loss in Cohesion
U.N. Capital Development Agencies (N = 32)	78%	--	44%	31%	87%	54%	-24%
Technical Assistance (N = 54)	100	80	63	33	100	64	-36
World Trading System (N = 46)	24	71	72	75	--	72	48
World Economic Development Plans (N = 12)	-3	18	100	--	--	48	51
Science and Technology (N = 68)	66	36	66	-9	100	46	-20
Trade/Development/ Science/Technology (N = 27)	57	57	73	29	86	60	3

Table 7

COHESION OF REGIONAL ORGANIZATION MEMBERS IN U.N. ROLL CALL
VOTING AFTER FORMATION OF REGIONAL GROUP: 1946-1968

(In percent; rank-ordered by cohesion on all U.N. issues)

Organization	Bloc Cohesion	
	All Issues	Economic Issues
Warsaw Pact (U.S.S.R. and East Europe)	95%	--
Comecon (U.S.S.R., Mongolia, and East Europe)	95	93%
EACSO/EACM (East Africa)	75	81
Benelux (Low Countries)	73	68
Conseil de l'Entente (West Africa)	70	67
Nordic Council (Scandinavia)	67	71
Arab League (Southwest Asia and North Africa)	67	66
EEC (Belgium, France, Germany, Italy, Luxembourg, Netherlands)	64	56
LAFTA (Latin America)	63	52
ODECA/CACM (Central America)	58	60
UAM/OAMCE/OCAM (West, Central, and East Africa)	55	60
ASA/ASEAN (Southeast Asia)	53	68
UDEAC (Central Africa)	44	76
OAS (U.S. and Latin America)	42	43
NATO	40	--
EFTA (Austria, Denmark, Norway, Portugal, Sweden, Switzerland, and U.K.)	38	31
Council of Europe (Essentially same as NATO)	37	38
OAU (Africa--except Union of South Africa)	36	69
OEEC/OECD (Essentially same as NATO)	35	38
RCD (Iran, Pakistan, Turkey)	32	52
SEATO (U.S., U.K., France, Southeast Asia)	16	--
Baghdad Pact/CENTO (U.S., U.K., and RCD)	2	--

League, and even such newcomers as the Customs Union of Central Africa (UDEAC) and the Organization of African Unity (OAU).

More useful for deciding between the alternative explanations suggested above is time-series evidence--the net gain or loss in bloc cohesion over time. Table 8 provides some summary indicators of this.

After 1951, as we have already observed, the ODECA/CACM countries increased their mean global voting cohesion by 26 percent more than did the United Nations as a whole; however, the gain on economic issues was a scant 3 percent more. Calculations for the LAFTA grouping (using 1961 as the cutoff) show an almost identical relative increase in cohesion (25 percent) across all issues, but they show an even poorer performance in agreeing on strictly economic issues (-7 percent). If one regards the "take-off point" for Central American integration as 1961 rather than 1951, the relative increase in cohesiveness of the Central Americans beyond that of their southern brethren appears even more significant. However, Table 8 suggests that much of the emergent global concordance of the Five may be related more to general regional trends than to specifically Common Market-related experiences.

In more macro-comparative terms, the cohesion of the CACM/ODECA group is very impressive. The OAS has been somewhat less cohesive than one would expect, given the early date of its founding. As concerns Comecon and the Warsaw Pact, their initially high levels of voting cohesion left little room for improvement. On the other hand, regional organizations like RCD and SEATO, which started at very low levels of international agreement, were able to show high relative rates of improvement rather easily.

To the extent that voting in the U.N. General Assembly provides a comprehensive, structured, and historically consistent context within which to measure countries' global foreign policy preferences indirectly (admittedly a risky assumption), the evidence supports the view that there has been some post-integration convergence on the part of the Central American countries. Two observations, however, call into question the inference that this trend is related to mutual regional experiences. On the one hand, the convergence is weakest in the issue arena (economics) most extensively handled at the regional level. On the other hand, substantially similar findings can be observed for the LAFTA and even the OAS regional groupings, where changes in the scope and level of mutual commitment have been--to put it mildly-- much less impressive. Succinctly stated, the Central Americans are not performing in a much more unified manner than their less regionally integrated continental brethren.

Clearly, the payoff for a five-member Central American bloc in a 120 plus-member U.N. General Assembly is low. At best,

Table 8

NET GAIN/LOSS OF COHESION OF REGIONAL ORGANIZATION MEMBERS
IN U.N. ROLL CALL VOTING AFTER FORMATION OF REGIONAL GROUP:
1946-1968

(In percent)

Organization[a]	Date Founded	Gain/Loss in Bloc Cohesion	
		All Issues	Economic Issues
ODECA/CACM	1951	26%	3%
LAFTA	1961	25	-7
OAS	1948	15	12
RCD	1965	14	36
EEC	1953	9	-20
Comecon	1949	8	-1
SEATO	1955	7	--
ASA/ASEAN	1962	5	9
Nordic Council	1953	4	-11
Warsaw Pact	1955	1	--
Baghdad Pact/CENTO	1956	-1	--
Council of Europe	1949	-3	-37
NATO	1949	-3	--
OEEC/OECD	1949	-5	-37
EFTA	1961	-10	-36
OAU	1964	-10	31
UDEAC	1964	-31	27

[a]For brief descriptive summaries of organizational memberships,
see Table 7 above.

NOTE: Several regional groupings have high cohesion scores but
do not permit a before/after comparison because they ante-
date the U.N. These include Benelux, Arab League, East
African Community, Conseil de l'Entente.

63

it might place concerted factional pressure on a larger Latin American--or even "Western"--group, and influence outcomes indirectly. In the 21-member Organization of American States, its combined five votes could count for much more.

Unfortunately, "rigorous political analyses of the Organization of American States (OAS) have been meager."[92] Studies of caucusing patterns, roll call votes, differentiation by issue areas, interpersonal influence, and organizational dynamics are lacking. Treatments have been historical and descriptive, if not legalistic, advocatory, or polemic. For our purposes, they also suffer from an exclusive focus upon the activities and motives of the United States and the Latin American "great powers."[93]

The lack of detailed studies of the OAS is not surprising, however. As Jerome Slater points out, the political process within the OAS is not as openly competitive and bloc-structured as in the United Nations: "Most OAS decisions are still the outcomes of painstakingly constructed compromises in which, to avoid open splits, strong efforts are made to accommodate even the weakest and smallest states and issues are rarely pushed to a vote before consensus is attained."[94] Behind this facade of inter-American harmony, of course, lie subtle exchanges of influence and deference, of great power hegemony and coalitional resistance, but they have yet to be satisfactorily documented.

An important reason for the very limited discussion of Central American participation in the OAS is, quite simply, that these countries have not played an innovative or aggressive role in the organization. They are among its most deferential members: "There has not been a single important vote in which a majority of the Central American and Caribbean states, so closely tied both politically and economically to Washington, has broken with the United States."[95] Certainly a political unification of the Five would make it more difficult for the U.S. State Department to muster the votes needed to block OAS resolutions or actions antithetic to U.S. interests.

---

[92]Slater, p. 3.

[93]This (understandable) preoccupation greatly diminishes the utility of Minerva Morales, A Majority of One (Beverly Hills: Sage Publications, 1970), and Gordon Connell-Smith, The Inter-American System (London: Oxford University Press, 1966), for our purposes.

[94]Slater, p. 26.

[95]Ibid.

However, the Central Americans have not been completely
passive and deferential to U.S. positions within the organization.
In the prewar period they collectively (but futilely) supported
the establishment of an Inter-American Court of Justice with
mandatory jurisdiction.[96] In 1954 Guatemala vainly sought,
against the united opposition of the other four, to bypass the
regional organization and place its case against Honduras, Nicaragua, and the United States directly before the United Nations.
Costa Rica has periodically sought to transform the OAS into an
"anti-dictatorial alliance," using it as forum for denouncing
tyrannical regimes and military seizures of power. Obviously,
this objective (expressed as late as 1963) could hardly have been
compatible with that of the Somoza regime next door. (Interest-
ingly, Costa Rica raised this issue before the OAS _after_ the
military coups in Honduras and Guatemala in 1963 and _after_ it had
joined the _Mercomún_. It withheld official recognition, but col-
laborated with these regimes in economic policy matters. On
succeeding occasions [in 1964 and 1965], when coups occurred
elsewhere, Costa Rica did _not_ raise the issue, indicating--
perhaps--a newly acquired political deference to its economic
partners.) Lacking an army of its own, Costa Rica has taken the
lead in proposing that the OAS take up the issue of regional arms
control. Only Chile and, for a brief period, Brazil have supported that initiative. However, in this instance, Costa Rica
has continued to press the issue despite a total lack of responsiveness from its regional partners.

Except for these spurts of activity, the Central American
countries have generally supported without reservation the prior
jurisdiction of regional over global collective security and the
conversion of the OAS into a U.S.-directed "anti-Communist alliance." They voted en bloc to expel Cuba from inter-American
institutions in 1961, accepted the U.S. blockade of the same
year, and supported the trade and diplomatic embargo of 1964.
In the Dominican crisis of 1965 they supplied five key votes
"collectively sanctioning" the prior, unilateral intervention
by the United States. Costa Rica, El Salvador, Honduras, and
Nicaragua subsequently sent small contingents of occupying troops.

Jerome Slater notes the emergence after the Cuban missile
crisis of increasingly militant "bloc" pressures on the part of
the Central American countries for OAS anti-Communist measures.
He argues that "the United States has not only ceased to exercise
'leadership' . . . but on the contrary in this matter has become
a force for _restraint_ within the inter-American system."[97] With

---

[96]Connell-Smith, pp. 96, 99.

[97]Slater, p. 141 (author's emphasis). Costa Rica rather dramatically changed its position. In 1960, it had expressed

the Central Americans clamoring for a break in relations and an economic boycott, threatening to walk out, and warning that they faced internal upheaval if nothing were done, and the "Outer Six" (Argentina, Brazil, Chile, Mexico, Bolivia, and Ecuador) resisting all punitive actions, the U.S. delegation found itself in a delicate situation.[98] These collective pressures in 1962 (and subsequent pressures in 1963 and 1964) imply the articulation of a genuinely regional policy on security matters distinctive from, although ultimately supportive of, that of the United States.

With this emergent "hard-line" stance on collective security issues, and with Costa Rica soft-pedalling its anti-dictatorial initiatives, Central American foreign policy-makers seem to have arrived at a convergent and rather independent stance in the OAS. (Field interviews with national foreign office personnel in 1967 substantiated this conclusion.) Many traced its origin to an informal agreement made at the tenth anniversary session of the United Nations in San Francisco to coordinate policy in all international organizations. Subsequent performance shows this effort to have been more successful in the OAS than in the United Nations. In the former, the Central Americans have acquired a separate "caucus capacity" which they have begun to use effectively to influence OAS elections[99] and economic policy deliberations.[100]

---

reservations about condemning the Cuban revolution; two years later it was proposing a "NATO-type" military alliance to include the United States, Colombia, Venezuela, the Caribbean, and the Central American states. (Ibid., pp. 141, 146.)

[98]The delegation extricated itself at the last moment when Haiti switched its vote to favor a watered-down "incompatibility" resolution excluding Cuban participation in inter-American organs. Reputedly, the change of heart cost the United States some $13 million in loans to Haiti (ibid., p. 156).

[99]According to newspaper accounts, the selection of the new Secretary-General was deadlocked for months over the intransigence of a small-state bloc, in which the Central Americans figured prominently. In a compromise outcome, a Salvadorean was elected Deputy Secretary-General, the first Central American to hold such a high post in the OAS. (See Benjamin Welles, "OAS Deadlock on Successor to Mora is Reported Broken," New York Times, 11 February 1968.)

[100]As noted above, Ministers of Economy and national and regional técnicos meet in advance of CIAP, CIES, CECLA, and other such deliberations, and usually present a united position. Here, of course, integrative learning is facilitated by the fact that the

This new external capacity is ambiguously related to integrative events elsewhere. At the "security community" level, it has clearly been the product of extra-regional and macro-systemic conditions, weakly legitimated and maintained by permanent organizational effort. Nor has ODECA provided a viable forum for more general foreign policy coordination--despite repeated resolutions to that effect. Only on the issue of united Central American support for the Guatemalan claim to sovereignty over Belice (British Honduras) is there evidence of some effective (if largely symbolic) collaboration. Economic policy-makers have been able to transfer their joint efforts to new issues and forums, but their effect on Ministers of Foreign Affairs and diplomats has been of the indirect, "fall-out" variety. The direct impact of increased external penetration seems to have led to greater "acquiescent" rather than "promotive" adaptation in these arenas. Before policy externalization can proceed much further and become regular "bloc" practice, it seems likely that certain institutional changes will be necessary at the national level. Traditionally, Central American delegations to international conferences have been rather loosely instructed.[101] Given the absense of organized publics at home sensitive to broader external issues, the practice of naming representatives as sinecures for personal friends or political enemies, the generally low salience of most foreign policy problems, the poor organization of the ministries themselves,[102] and (of course) the endemic instability of domestic policy-makers, the performance of Central Americans in external forums has been uncertain, individualistic, technically ill-equipped, subject to frequent changes, and very unevenly implemented at home--as witness the ratification of the OAS and ILO conventions. Changes in recruitment, professional train-

---

actors in the Central American, Latin American, Pan-American, and global contexts are the same. Also of importance are the growing number of occasions (e.g., the 1967 Punta del Este summit) in which Ministers of Economy or their representatives attend jointly with Ministers of Foreign Affairs. This sort of inter-ministerial contact had been infrequent at the regional level.

[101]John Martz records that Somoza's instructions to his ambassador (and brother-in-law) in Washington were always the same: "Cooperate fully with the delegation of the United States of America" (Martz, p. 199).

[102]The Guatemalan Foreign Office has by far the best reputation in the area for organizational and intellectual strength, and Guatemala has the area's most independent and consistent (until very recently) voting record in international organizations.

ing,[103] and organized support--at the national level--will probably have to precede any durable acquisition of a capacity for
regional foreign policy-making. At the present juncture (barring
any sudden changes in national political orientation), there do
not appear to be any substantive policy differences between the
Five which would prevent it--only a heavy patina of international
and inter-institutional rivalry, mistrust, and jealousy.

The unexpected "Football War" between El Salvador and
Honduras in July 1969 has irrevocably altered the future of the
integration process. Its very occurrence, of course, demonstrated
the fragility of the "security community," which seemed to have
been externally imposed upon the region. As one Central American
friend put it, "We suddenly learned to our great surprise that we
could go to war without first getting permission from the U.S.
ambassador." ODECA, caught in the midst of its perennial stalemate over the selection of a Secretary-General, played no effective role. Military "unification" by CONDECA was clearly revealed
as an operation opportunistically designed to attract U.S. support
and suppress domestic opposition, but irrelevant to the maintenance of regional peace and security. The institutions of economic integration, with their surrounding clienteles of national
técnicos and empresarios, proved incapable of stopping the out-
break of hostilities. Their deliberately apolitical, segmental
strategy weakened their capacity to influence policy outcomes
in other issue "compartments"--e.g., mobility of persons--and
left them short of needed allies, especially in the politico-
military sector, when the "crunch" came. Upon the cessation of
hostilities, however, these institutions played a major role in
the efforts to pick up the pieces. Ironically, they would have
found their authority considerably strengthened if some new modus
operandi had been negotiated.[104] Subsequently, the search for
an interim arrangement collapsed, and Central American institutions are currently (Spring 1972) almost inoperative. Honduras
continues to boycott all Salvadorean trade, and has blockaded its

---

[103]Guatemala has recently announced its intentions to open a
Central American institute for the training of diplomats and
foreign office personnel.

[104]For a detailed account of the sequence of activities aimed
at piecing together a new package-deal which would substantially
expand the level of authority, as well as the scope, of regional
institutions, see SIECA, Carta Informativa, Nos. 99-109 (January-
November 1970), and "Central America: The Recovery of Regional
Relations," B.O.L.S.A. Review, 4 (December 1970), pp. 672-676.

frontier to the passage of Salvadorean goods to Nicaragua and
Costa Rica. Early in 1971 it withdrew altogether from the Mercomún.[105]

The norm of reciprocity concerning mutual toleration of
domestic political systems has been broken, and the immediate
result will inevitably be a return to the status quo ante in
terms of foreign policy. The paramount objective is again likely
to become the maintenance of "compatible" neighbors--by any means
possible. More important, the armed conflict unleashed intense
and implacably antagonistic nationalistic sentiments between the
two protagonists--far exceeding the more symbolic negative stereo-
typing endemic in previous Honduran-Salvadorean relations and,
indeed, throughout the region. This political mobilization of
hostile sentiment is unprecedented in extent and protractedness
within Central America. It may become contagious, although the
specific grounds for mutual antagonism that exist between Honduras
and El Salvador are not replicated elsewhere in the region. At
a minimum, a new rhetoric stressing national traits, exclusive
advantage, and great sensitivity to benefits accruing to neighbors
has been widely promulgated, and may make it difficult for "non-
combatants" to defer benefits or accept compromise solutions in
the name of Central American-ness.

In this renewed atmosphere of bilateralism, shifting
alliances, accelerated arms purchases, courting of "interested"
extra-regional powers, and intervention in the internal politics
of one's regional "partners," policy externalization is hardly
likely to increase. Indeed it is doubtful if previously negotiated, "established" positions on segmented economic issues can
be maintained. Foreign policy-makers will be forced to devote
most of their attention to more proximate and immediate "strategic" needs within the region. Domestic politicians are likely
to seek to avoid at all costs any apparent concessions to "geno-
cidal" enemies. Some may use protracted external struggle and
exacerbated patriotism as an excuse for distracting attention
from long overdue internal reforms and for practicing continuismo
(self-perpetuation in power). In addition, one of the prime
pressures for policy coordination vis-à-vis outsiders may decline
as private foreign capitalists hesitate to make investments in
such an uncertain environment. To the extent that foreign public
actors (e.g., the U.S. Department of State or Defense) are held
responsible for having caused defeat or prevented victory (or
both), their intrusive capacity is likely to diminish.

---

[105]The best source for following the so far fruitless attempts
at re-establishing Mercomún institutions is the "Informe mensual
de la integración latinoamericana," Comércio Exterior (México,
D.F.). A useful summary can be found in the July 1971 issue, pp.
568-575.

Chapter 6

CONCLUSIONS

Even if exacerbated nationalism, shift in focus of political attention, rigidification in domestic politics, decay of
regional institutional authority, isolation of regional técnicos,
and decrease in the rate of external penetration lead one to very
pessimistic predictions about the future of policy externalization
(or, for that matter, forecasts of the future of integration itself), we can derive some useful conclusions from the performance
of the first six to seven years of the CACM. I would group these
conclusions into two categories: (I) those specifically relevant
to Central America and (II) those relevant to contemporary integration efforts in general.

I. Central American Integration

Certain peculiarities of the Central American setting
seem to inhibit policy externalization among its five countries:

(1) The grossly assymetric and cumulative nature of
dependence of the region upon a single external actor means that
on virtually any issue, policy externalization involves "taking
on" the United States. Were their external relations more diver-
sified, Central Americans could begin learning cooperative habits
in "minor leagues"--forums where they have greater potential in-
fluence--and only later transfer them to the "big leagues." To
a certain extent, negotiations with Mesoamerican and Caribbean
neighbors might perform this function, but no deals made at this
level are likely to be sufficiently important to provide the
needed basis of institutional self-confidence and public visibility.

(2) The natural object of externalization--the United
States--has responded with great policy flexibility. Less char-
itably, one might say it has played a complex double game. On
the one hand, it has accepted--even promoted--multilateralization,
while penetrating the institutions that articulate this position,
thereby diminishing their potential aggressiveness; on the other
hand, it has maintained and even expanded bilateral channels in
order to protect its economic and security interests separately
within each national polity. On no occasion has the United States
unequivocably insisted on collective deliberation or refused to
recognize individual appeals, as it did, for example, in the case

of the Marshall Plan. This, plus the proliferation of subsidies for a polycentric set of regional institutions, suggests (but by no means proves) that U.S. authorities have deliberately sought to discourage the development of an externalization capacity. In any case, they certainly haven't consciously made it any easier.

(3) The diminutive size of the Central American countries seriously limits their capacity to exert influence. Even if they were to merge their economies completely, the resultant market would be no larger than that of Peru. Granted that the special strategic location of Central America gives it considerable "nuisance value," so that as a unit it might play a somewhat more important world role than Peru, nevertheless that would hardly seem to justify a heavy and risky political investment. (A recent comparative study on "subordinate state systems," in which one might have expected the Central American integration movement to figure prominently, haughtily dismisses it on the grounds that "were political integration to occur among such nations . . . they would have a similar position in their subordinate systems . . . as they do now, even though their power within the system would be increased."[106] Again, it is hard to justify a substantial effort simply to establish a more cohesive factional capacity within a larger regional grouping, itself of dubious import in international politics.)

(4) The levels of national political complexity and participation (political development, if you wish) within the region restrict its capacity for policy externalization. We have already noted the inhibiting effects of sinecure-ridden, inefficient, disorganized national foreign ministries, and an ingrained tradition of "acquiescent adaptation." Perhaps more important in the long run is the relative absence of linkages between wider publics in mass organizations and political parties and foreign policy decision-makers. Where associational linkages do exist, they are dominated by narrow sectoral interests wedded to the externally dependent status quo. New and more aggressive defense of regional interests is hardly likely to be forthcoming from collaboration among these groups alone. Only by shifting their supportive alliance and appealing to wider publics--i.e., only by politicizing the integration movement--can regional reform-mongers cultivate a spill-over into this domain. Massive illiteracy, low levels of political information, personalistic loyalties and leadership styles, erratic partisan competitiveness, and systematic repression of opponents make such an expansive tactic risky, if not impossible. At the present levels of political development,

---

[106]Louis J. Cantori and Steven L. Spiegel, eds., The International Politics of Regions: A Comparative Approach (Englewood Cliffs: Prentice-Hall, 1970), p. 6 [fn. 7].

there is little alternative but to rely upon more specialized, elitist publics.

Related to these structural conditions are the limited legitimacy and endemic instability of the Central American polities, with the exception of Costa Rica. The leaders' preoccupation with survival leads them to make excessively short-term calculations of interest. Even if técnicos could marshal convincing evidence that the long-term interest--even survival--of regional development and integration depends upon such "externalizations" as the regulation of foreign capital, joint protection and promotion of commodity trade, coordination of foreign aid for infrastructure, etc., embattled dominant elites are not likely to forego any immediately available, bilateral payoffs. Policy externalization in Central America seems to depend on some prior successful politicization of integration objectives, and this, in turn, depends on some prior changes in political structure and stability. Unfortunately for the proponents of regionalism, changes at this level are beyond their manipulative capacity.[107] By the time they occur, the region's resources and institutions may be so permanently penetrated by outside forces as to make their recovery by indigenous interests impossible.

Conversely, where such prior changes in political mass mobilization are sponsored from above by dominant elites around nationalistic-populist goals, they make consensual, incremental reform-mongering at the regional level impossible, without necessarily leading to a decrease in dependence upon extra-regional powers (rhetoric to the contrary notwithstanding).

II. General Conclusions

In addition to conclusions about conditions "peculiar" to the Central American region, a number of more "general" observations concerning policy externalization can be induced from our analysis:

(1) There is clear and impressive evidence that regional integration has stimulated efforts at penetration by public and private external agents, and this has created pressures upon regional actors to respond collectively. Despite the fact that they have expanded the de facto scope of their deliberations beyond original commitment and expectation, these responses have been scattered over a variety of uncoordinated institutions and

---

[107]For more detailed speculation about such sequences of change at the national and regional levels, see my "A Revised Theory of Regional Integration."

have yet to result in a definitive increase in the level of regional authority. Instead, national authorities have tended to
use these newly acquired regional institutions episodically and
expediently. Depending on the external issue at stake, they have
turned to different regional actors and used their superior expertise and status (often granting them considerable autonomy in
formulating the joint position), but have hesitated to devolve
decisional autonomy upon them. Once the specific negotiations
were over, foreign policy-making returned securely to the national domain.

The linkage between expansive tendencies in the scope and
level of intra-regional policy and externalization seems rather
weak. Despite awareness and reform-mongering efforts by técnicos
and manifest engrenage-type pressures from national entrepreneurial and intellectual circles, major external issues have been
avoided; lesser ones have been handled in an ad hoc manner. One
reason seems to be the ingrained conservatism of foreign minis-
tries--their tendency to think in rigidly national terms, their
zealous defense of institutional prerogatives, and hence their resistance to integrative learning effects. Another reason is that
external representation has always been the hallmark of sovereignty. It is a highly symbolic and emotion-laden affair in which it
is difficult to divide competences and payoffs satisfactorily.[108]
The international status returns from effective regional collaboration are as yet not very salient, and can hardly compete with
the prestige which can be gleaned from the publicized pursuit of
exclusively national interests. Also, a distinctive regional
identity has been very slow and uneven in its development, and is
a long way from providing the affective, pseudo-gemeinschaftlich
sentiment to be gained from domestic nationalism. In short, all
of the regional change processes discussed in the introduction
to this work, and at greater length in my article "A Revised
Theory of Regional Integration," were either too weak to have
sustained policy externalization at this point in the integration
process or, in the case of inequity in the perceived distribution
of benefits, too strong to be overcome. The Honduran reaction

---

[108]These observations closely parallel those of Werner Feld in
his excellent study of externalization in The European Common
Market and the World (Englewood Cliffs: Prentice-Hall, 1967).
Despite his hypothesis that "the level of tension and strain built
in the external policy making process will be raised further until
such time that common policies have been developed which fulfill
the conditions the internal market requires for its effective
functioning" (p. 55), Feld finds a "persistent inclination of
individual member states to pursue independently their own foreign
policy goals rather than to submit to common procedures and common
objectives under Community auspices" (p. 161).

to the Fiscal Incentives Protocol is a fine example of the latter
process at work.

(2) Policy externalization is a less likely outcome where
the integrating units are set in a matrix of overlapping and competing international systems and subsystems.[109] Instead of being
left to their own devices within the same consistent institutional
context, national actors are faced with a multiple schedule of
opportunities and potential allies. The incentives for collaboration are bound to be different at the global (UN, IMF, IBRD,
GATT), the Pan-American (OAS, CIES, CIAP, IADB), or the Latin
American (ECLA, CECLA) levels, not to mention such embryonic
subsystems as the Mesoamerican or Caribbean. Differences are
likely to arise over the appropriate institutional forum for
action and over the feasibility of combining with different sets
of extra-regional actors.[110] Much that might have contributed
to a distinctively Central American position has been subsumed
within a larger Latin American stance. No matter how advisable
this strategy may be, it robs the region of an important impetus
for externalization.

(3) To the extent that integration in the contemporary
context tends to involve intense sensitivity to reciprocity of

---

[109]The effect of "partial systems" and organizational overlap
upon externalization was originally explored in Stanley Hoffmann,
"Discord in Community: The North Atlantic Area as a Partial International System" in F.O. Wilcox and H.F. Haviland, Jr., eds.,
The Atlantic Community: Progress and Prospects (New York:
Praeger, 1963), pp. 3-31; see also the treatment in Kaiser, pp.
102-106, where a hypothesis somewhat contradictory to the one
suggested here is advanced.

[110]I cannot resist quoting Stanley Hoffmann's ingenious meta-
phor: "Those nations that coexist in the same apparently separate 'home' of a geographic region find themselves both exposed
to the smells and noises that come from outside through all their
windows and doors, and looking at the outlying houses from which
the interference issues. Coming from diverse pasts, moved by
diverse tempers, living in different parts of the house, ines-
capably yet differently subjected and attracted to the outside
world, those cohabitants react unevenly to their exposure and cal-
culate differently how they could either reduce the disturbance
or affect in turn all those who live elsewhere" ("Obstinate or
Obsolete? The Fate of the Nation-State and the Case of Western
Europe" in Joseph S. Nye, Jr., ed., International Regionalism
[Boston: Little, Brown, 1968], p. 180).

benefits, "balanced development," and equality of participation,[111] externalization is made more difficult. Such a preoccupation more or less guarantees that the jointly elaborated positions will be based on a lowest common denominator calculation, held down by the most recalcitrant member. Special bilateral links with outsiders can be manipulated easily to block regional agreement. Most important, however, this sensitivity rules out a "Bismarckian" strategy, which would combine regional integration with an aggressive foreign policy. The structural requirement for this is the existence of a "core area"--a sub-region or member-state with a clear economic and political preeminence. It concentrates resources, redistributes some of them to peripheral areas within the region, and expends much of them in the promotion of external goals.[112] For better or worse, Central American integrators have rejected this approach--partly because hegemonic attempts have failed so dismally in the past. Elsewhere, I have shown that this region has a marked incongruence in the rank orderings of a number of indicators of relative size/power, and argued that this is likely to facilitate decision-making at the regional level: "Integrative arrangements in which a single member scores highest on all measures of potential size and power are more likely to run into severe distributional problems. Winning and losing statuses are easier to assign; package deals based on differential rates of return (and differential perceptions) are harder to negotiate."[113] Whatever it may do for intra-regional policy, equality and dispersion in power make it more difficult to elaborate extra-regional positions and to mobilize resources for their defense.

---

[111]See E.B. Haas and P.C. Schmitter, The Politics of Economics in Latin American Regionalism (Denver: University of Denver Monograph, 1965), and "Economics and Differential Patterns of Political Integration," International Organization, XVIII (Autumn 1964), pp. 705-37; also Hansen, Central America, pp. 56-64. For a discussion (and rejection) of "integración hegemónica" within Central America, see Francisco Villagrán Kramer, "Presentación del tema central" in Aspectos sociales y políticos de la integración centroamericana (Guatemala, C.A.: Editorial José de Pineda Ibarra, 1970), pp. 66-67.

[112]Deutsch et al., pp. 72, 137-139.

[113]"Further Notes on Operationalizing Some Variables Related to Regional Integration," International Organization, XXIII (Spring 1969), pp. 327-331. Comparing rank incongruence of size/power indicators in 1960 and 1965 by means of Kendall's coefficient of concordance showed, however, a clear net increase in Central America in the consistency of winning and losing statuses. By inference this should make decision-making increasingly difficult.

Returning to the contending "schools of thought" described in the Introduction, we find that they all correctly anticipated some developments. As the Marxists predicted, regional trade liberalization stimulated penetration by foreign private capital and hegemonic political systems, and the ensuing benefits of integration were unevenly distributed. Yet the region as a whole seemed to be diversifying its sources of economic dependence and beginning to assert, for the first time, some political independence both in the global and hemispheric arenas. The Reformists may derive some comfort from the evidence that countervailing processes exist which can be exploited by the standard neo-functional strategic gambits of indirection, incrementalism, package-dealing, and crisis-manipulation, but they can scarcely derive any satisfaction from the global outcome. Although largely for reasons beyond the Reformists' control, their carefully laid plans were swept aside by the political force which lies at the center of the third "school of thought": domestic nationalism. Clearly, in contemporary Central America, no attainable combination of material payoffs or affective satisfactions at the regional level can compete with the mobilizational capacity of nationalism. Until this force is "domesticated"--i.e., converted into viable representative institutions and legitimate political authority and, thereby, stripped of at least some of its mass explosiveness and irrationality--no attempt, no matter how carefully contrived, at regional community formation is likely to succeed. The danger, however, is not that national governments are in any imminent danger of being reduced to functioning "principally on the technical level," as Furtado puts it, but that opportunistic nationalist leaders will mobilize their captive clienteles from above in the interests of self-perpetuation in power and, in the process, leave behind both a residue of antagonism which will make future regional consolidation much more difficult and a legacy of public policy which will increase rather than decrease their country's dependence on external powers.

If the Central American experience can be taken as generally paradigmatic for economic integration movements which rely primarily upon private enterprise and unregulated market forces, and which are composed of small, underdeveloped, assymetrically-dependent states, more or less equal in their impotence, then I would conclude that one of the more likely political consequences of such movements will be to provide a strong impetus for external penetration and a much weaker one for policy externalization. They are, therefore, likely to lead to alienation of domestic resources in the short run; the long-run countervalence of dialectical effects seems to depend on prior changes in national political systems which are beyond the direct control of regional reform-mongers. (One could argue that the increased intrusion

of external agents will make these prior political changes even
less likely to occur.)

If, in this context, regional integration by itself is
not likely to contribute to a progressive redistribution of
wealth and human resources, to a greater dispersion of political
power and democratic accountability, or to a lesser dependence
upon hegemonic outsiders--or if regional integration is exceedingly vulnerable to rapid and unpredictable crystallizations of mass
nationalist sentiment--then "¿Para qué entonces, la integración
centroamericana?" ("Why bother with Central American integration?")[114] The increasing frequency with which Central Americans
have begun to ask this question could be cause for optimism if
we believe, with Karl Marx, that societies raise only those issues
which they stand some chance of resolving.

---

[114]For a similar conclusion, reached by taking a different
route, see Edelberto Torre-Rivas, "Problemas del desarrollo y
la dependencia en Centroamérica," Revista Mexicana de Sociología,
XXXI (April-June 1969), pp. 223-243. See also the brilliant
synthesis in Kramer, pp. 51-84.

GLOSSARY OF ACRONYMS

AID:	Agency for International Development
CABEI:	Central American Bank for Economic Integration
CACM:	Central American Common Market
CCE:	Committee for Economic Cooperation of the Central American Isthmus
CECLA:	Special Commission for Latin American Coordination
CIAP:	Inter-American Council of the Alliance for Progress
CIES:	Inter-American Economic and Social Council
COCESNA:	Central American Air Navigation Services Corporation
CONDECA:	Central American Defense Council
CSUCA:	Superior University Council of Central America
EACM:	East African Common Market
ECLA:	United Nations Economic Commission for Latin America
EEC:	European Economic Community
ESAPAC:	Central American School of Public Administration
FAO:	Food and Agriculture Organization
FECAICA:	Central American Federation of Chambers and Associations of Industry
FEDECAME:	Coffee Federation of America
GATT:	General Agreement on Tariffs and Trade
IADB:	Inter-American Development Bank
IBRD:	International Bank for Reconstruction and Development
ICA:	International Coffee Agreement
ICAITI:	Central American Institute of Research and Industrial Technology
ICAO:	International Civil Aviation Organization
ICAP:	Central American Institute of Public Administration
IMF:	International Monetary Fund
INCAP:	Institute of Nutrition of Central America and Panama
INTAL:	Institute for the Integration of Latin America

JOPLAN:	Joint Planning Mission
LAFTA:	Latin American Free Trade Association
Mercomún:	Term commonly used to refer to the Central American Common Market
OAS:	Organization of American States
OAU:	Organization of African Unity
ODECA:	Organization of Central American States
ROCAP:	Regional Office for Central America and Panama Affairs
SIECA:	Permanent Secretariat of the General Treaty on Central American Integration
UDEAC:	Customs Union of Central Africa
UNCTAD:	United Nations Conference on Trade and Development

BIBLIOGRAPHY

Alliance for Progress. Report on Central American National De-
velopment Plans and the Process of Economic Integration.
Washington, D.C.: Committee of Nine, Alliance for Progress,
August 1966.

Almeida, Romulo, et al. Factores para la integración latinoamericana. México: Fondo de Cultura Económica, 1966.

Anderson, Charles A. "Politics and Development Policy in Central
America," Midwest Journal of Political Science, V (November
1961).

Aragão, José María. "Integración, dependencia y desarrollo:
Reflexiones en torno de 'Sub-desarrollo y estancamiento en
América Latina,'" Revista de la Integración, No. 1 (November
1967).

Ball, M. Margaret. "Bloc Voting in the General Assembly,"
International Organization, V (February 1951).

Barber, W., and Ronning, C.N. International Security and Military
Power. Columbus: Ohio State University Press, 1966.

Bennaton, J. Abraham. El Mercado Común Centroamericano: Su
evolución y perspectivas. Tegucigalpa: Tesis, Universidad
Autonoma de Honduras, Facultad de Ciencias Económicas,
September 1964.

B.O.L.S.A. Review, various issues.

CABEI. "Bases para la formulación de una política regional en
materia de fomento de inversiones." Tegucigalpa, March
1965; mimeo.

Cable, Vincent. "The 'Football War' and the Central American
Common Market," International Affairs, 43 (October 1969).

Cantori, Louis J., and Spiegel, Steven L., eds. The International
Politics of Regions: A Comparative Approach. Englewood
Cliffs: Prentice-Hall, 1970.

Castillo, Carlos. Growth and Integration in Central America.
New York: Praeger, 1966.

Cochrane, James D. The Politics of Regional Integration: The
Central American Case. New Orleans: Tulane University
Press, 1969.

_____. "U.S. Attitudes Towards Central American Economic
Integration," Inter-American Economic Affairs, 18 (Autumn
1964).

Connell-Smith, Gordon. The Inter-American System. London: Oxford University Press, 1966.

Dell, Sidney. "Obstacles to Latin American Integration" in R. Hilton, ed., The Movement Toward Latin American Unity. New York: Praeger, 1969.

Denham, Robert E. "The Role of the U.S. as an External Actor in the Integration of Latin America," Journal of Common Market Studies, VII (March 1969).

Denton, Charles F. "Interest Groups in Panama and the Central American Common Market," Inter-American Economic Affairs, 21 (1967).

Deutsch, Karl. "External Influences on the Internal Behavior of States" in R. Barry Farrell, ed., Approaches to Comparative and International Politics. Evanston: Northwestern University Press, 1966.

_____, et al. Political Community in the North Atlantic Area. Princeton: Princeton University Press, 1957.

Dillon, C. Douglas. "An Integrated Program of Development for Latin America," Department of State Bulletin, XXXIX (December 8, 1958).

ECLA. Evaluación de la integración económica en Centroamérica. New York: United Nations, 1966.

Eisenhower, Milton S. The Wine is Bitter. Garden City, N.Y.: Doubleday, 1963.

Fagan, Stuart. Central American Economic Integration: The Politics of Unequal Benefits. Berkeley: Institute of International Studies, University of California, 1970. [Research Series, No. 15]

Feld, Werner. The European Common Market and the World. Englewood Cliffs: Prentice-Hall, 1967.

Ferrer, Aldo. "Empresario, integración y desarrollo," Los Empresarios y la integración de América Latina. Buenos Aires: INTAL, 1967.

Furtado, Celso. "U.S. Hegemony and the Future of Latin America" in Irving L. Horowitz et al., eds., Latin American Radicalism. New York: Vintage Books, 1969.

Galtung, Johan. "A Structural Theory of Aggression," Journal of Peace Research, 2 (1964).

Goodwin, Geoffrey. "The Expanding United Nations, I--Voting Patterns," International Affairs, 36 (April 1960).

Gosovic, Branislav. "UNCTAD: North-South Encounter," International Conciliation, No. 568 (May 1968).

Grunwald, Joseph. "Latin American Economic Development and the

United States" in A.M. Piedra, ed., Socio-Economic Change in Latin America. Washington, D.C.: Catholic University Press, 1970.

Guerra Borges, A., and Mora Valverde, E. "Some Problems of the Economic Integration of Central America," World Marxist Review, 5 (June 1956).

Haas, Ernst B. Beyond the Nation-State. Stanford: Stanford University Press, 1964.

_____, and Schmitter, P.C. The Politics of Economics in Latin American Regionalism. Denver: University of Denver Monograph, 1965.

_____, and _____. "Economics and Differential Patterns of Political Integration," International Organization, XVIII (Autumn 1964).

Hansen, Roger D. Central America: Regional Integration and Economic Development. Washington, D.C.: National Planning Association, 1967.

_____. "Regional Integration: Reflections on a Decade of Theoretical Efforts," World Politics, 21 (January 1969).

Harrison, S. Lorenzo. "Central American Dilemma: National Sovereignty or Unification," International Review of History and Political Science, 2 (December 1965).

Herrera, Felipe. Nacionalismo latinoamericano. Santiago: Editorial Universitaria, 1967.

_____. Nacionalismo, regionalismo, internacionalismo. Buenos Aires: INTAL, 1970.

Hoffman, Stanley. "Discord in Community: The North Atlantic Area as a Partial International System" in F.O. Wilcox and H.F. Haviland, Jr., eds., The Atlantic Community: Progress and Prospects. New York: Praeger, 1963.

_____. "Obstinate or Obsolete? The Fate of the Nation-State and the Case of Western Europe" in Joseph S. Nye, Jr., ed., International Regionalism. Boston: Little, Brown, 1968.

Houston, John S. Latin America in the United Nations. New York: Carnegie Endowment, 1956.

Hovet, Thomas, Jr. Bloc Politics in the United Nations. Cambridge: Harvard University Press, 1960.

Hovey, Harold A. United States Military Assistance: A Study of Policies and Practices. New York: Praeger, 1965.

Hunter, William. "Central American Producers Unite to Push Cotton," Cotton International, 1967.

Jaguaribe, Hélio. "Coordinación de las políticas nacionales" in Romulo Almeida et al., Factores para la integración latino-americana. México: Fondo de Cultura Económica, 1966.

Jiménez Lazcano, Mauro. Integración económica e imperialismo. México: Editorial Nuestro Tiempo, 1968.

Johnson, H. The Bay of Pigs. New York: Dell Publishing Co., Inc., 1964.

JOPLAN. "Centroamérica: Lineamientos para una política de desarrollo regional." Guatemala, C.A., September 1964; mimeo.

Kaiser, Karl. "The U.S. and the EEC in the Atlantic System: The Problem of Theory," Journal of Common Market Studies, V (June 1967).

Kaplan, Marcos. Problemas del desarrollo y de la integración en América Latina. Caracas: Monte Avila Editores, 1968.

Kramer, Francisco Villagrán. "Presentación del tema central" in Aspectos sociales y políticos de la integración centroamericana. Guatemala, C.A.: Editorial José de Pineda Ibarra, 1970.

Lagos, Gustavo. International Stratification and Underdeveloped Countries. Chapel Hill: University of North Carolina Press, 1963.

Lijphart, Arend. "The Analysis of Bloc Voting in the General Assembly: A Critique and Proposal," American Political Science Review, LVII (December 1963).

Lizano F., Eduardo. El Mercado Común y la distribución del ingreso. San José: Editorial Universitaria Centroamericana, 1969.

Loftus, Joseph E. "Latin American Defense Expenditures, 1938-1965," RAND Memorandum, RM-5310-PR/ISA (January 1968).

Martz, John. Central America. Chapel Hill: University of North Carolina Press, 1959.

May, Stacy, and Plaza, Galo. The United Fruit Company in Latin America. Washington, D.C.: National Planning Association, 1958.

McCamant, John F. Development Assistance in Central America. New York: Praeger, 1968.

McClelland, Donald H. "The Common Market's Contributions to Central American Economic Growth: A First Approximation" in R. Hilton, ed., The Movement Toward Latin American Unity. New York: Praeger, 1969.

Mecham, J. Lloyd. A Survey of United States-Latin American Relations. Boston: Houghton Mifflin, 1965.

Mikesell, Raymond. "External Financing and Regional Integration" in Miguel S. Wionczek, ed., Latin American Economic Integration. New York: Praeger, 1966.

Mitrany, David. A Working Peace System. Chicago: Quadrangle
Books, 1966.

Morales, Minerva. A Majority of One. Beverly Hills: Sage
Publications, 1970.

Nye, Joseph S., Jr. "Central American Regional Integration,"
International Conciliation, No. 562 (March 1967).

_____. "Comparative Regional Integration: Concept and
Measurement," International Organization, XXII (Autumn 1968).

_____. "Patterns and Catalysts in Regional Integration,"
International Organization, XIX (Autumn 1965).

Perroux, Francois. "Quién integra? En beneficio de quién se
realiza la integración?," Revista de la Integración, No. 1
(November 1967).

Powell, John D. "Military Assistance and Militarism in Latin
America," Western Political Quarterly, Vol. XVIII (June 1965).

Ramsett, David E. Regional Industrial Development in Central
America. New York: Praeger, 1969.

Riggs, Robert. Politics in the United Nations. Urbana: University of Illinois Press, 1958.

Rosenau, James. "Pre-Theories and Theories of Foreign Policy"
in R. Barry Farrell, ed., Approaches to Comparative and
International Politics. Evanston: Northwestern University
Press, 1966.

_____. "The Adaptation of National Societies: A Theory of
Political System Behavior and Transformation." New York:
McCaleb-Seiler, 1970.

Rosenthal, Gert K. "Algunos apuntes sobre la inversión extranjera
directa en el Mercado Común Centroamericano," INTAL (Buenos
Aires), Sem. 11/dt. 6, November 17, 1969.

Russett, Bruce. International Regions and the International
System. Chicago: Rand McNally, 1967.

Saxe-Fernandez, John. "The Central American Defense Council and
Pax Americana" in Irving L. Horowitz, Josué de Castro, and
John Gerassi, eds., Latin American Radicalism. New York:
Vintage Books, 1969.

Schmitter, Philippe C. "Central American Integration: Spill-
Over, Spill-Around or Encapsulation?," Journal of Common
Market Studies, IX, 1 (September 1970).

_____. "Further Notes on Operationalizing Some Variables
Related to Regional Integration," International Organization,
XXIII (Spring 1969).

_____. "A Revised Theory of Regional Integration," Inter-
national Organization, XXIV (Autumn 1970).

_____. "Three Neo-Functional Hypotheses about Regional Integration," International Organization, XXIII (Winter 1969).

Seward, F.H. "The Changing Balance of Power in the United Nations," The Political Quarterly, 28 (October-December 1957).

SIECA. Carta Informativa, various issues.

_____. Informe sobre los avances del programa de integración economica centroamericana, Febrero de 1966, Mayo de 1967. Guatemala, C.A., 1967; mimeo.

_____. "Nota de Secretaría sobre inversiones extranjeras." Guatemala, C.A., June 1965; mimeo.

Slater, Jerome. The OAS and United States Foreign Policy. Columbus: Ohio State University Press, 1967.

Teubal, Miguel. "The Failure of Latin America's Economic Integration" in James Petras and Maurice Zeitlin, eds., Latin America: Reform or Revolution? New York: Fawcett Books, 1968.

Teune, Henry. "The Learning of Integrative Habits" in P.E. Jacob and J.V. Toscano, eds., The Integration of Political Communities. Philadelphia: J.B. Lippincott, 1964.

Tobis, David. "The Central American Common Market: The Integration of Underdevelopment," NACLA Newsletter, III (January 1970).

Torre-Rivas, Edelberto. "Problemas del desarrollo y la dependencia en Centroamérica," Revista Mexicana de Sociología, XXXI (April-June 1969).

U.S. Department of Defense, Office of the Assistant Secretary of Defense for International Security Affairs. Military Assistance Facts. Washington, D.C., 1969.

U.S. House of Representatives, Committee on Appropriations, Subcommittee on Foreign Operations and Related Agencies. Foreign Assistance and Related Agencies Appropriations for 1971, Part I. Washington, D.C.: Government Printing Office, 1970.

_____, Committee on Foreign Affairs, Subcommittee on Inter-American Affairs. Central America: Some Observations on Its Common Market, Binational Centers and Housing Programs. Washington, D.C.: Government Printing Office, August 4, 1966.

Urquidi, Victor L. Free Trade and Economic Integration in Latin America. Berkeley: University of California Press, 1962.

Wionczek, Miguel S. "Condiciones de una integración viable" in Wionczek, ed., Integración de América Latina. México: Fondo de Cultura Económica, 1964.

_____. "Experiences of the Central American Economic Integration Program as Applied to East Africa," Industrialization and Productivity, 11 (1968).

_____. "La integración económica latinoamericana y la inversión privada extranjera," Comercio Exterior, XX (September 1970).

_____. "Latin American Integration and United States Economic Policies" in R.W. Gregg, ed., International Organization in the Western Hemisphere. Syracuse: Syracuse University Press, 1968.

_____. "La reaccion norteamericana ante el trato común a los capitales extranjeros en el Grupo Andino," Comercio Exterior, May 1971.

RESEARCH SERIES PUBLICATIONS

1. *The Chinese Anarchist Movement,* by R. Scalapino and G. T. Yu. ($1.00)
5. *Mexico and Latin American Economic Integration,* by Philippe C. Schmitter and Ernst B. Haas. ($1.00)
7. *Birth Rates in Latin America,* by O. A. Collver. ($2.50)
8. *Land Tenure and Taxation in Nepal, Volume III, The Jagir, Rakam, and Kipat Tenure Systems,* by Mahesh C. Regmi. ($2.50)
10. *Urban Areas in Indonesia: Administrative and Census Concepts,* by Pauline Dublin Milone. ($3.25)
12. *Land Tenure and Taxation in Nepal, Volume IV, Religious and Charitable Land Endowments: Guthi Tenure,* by Mahesh C. Regmi. ($2.75)
13. *The Pink Yo-Yo: Occupational Mobility in Belgrade, ca. 1915–1965,* by Eugene A. Hammel. ($2.00)
14. *Community Development in Israel and The Netherlands: A Comparative Analysis,* by Ralph M. Kramer. ($2.50)
15. *Central American Economic Integration,* by Stuart I. Fagan. ($1.75)
16. *The International Imperatives of Technology: Technological Change and the International Political System,* by E. B. Skolnikoff. ($2.95)

POLITICS OF MODERNIZATION SERIES PUBLICATIONS

1. *Spanish Bureaucratic-Patrimonialism in America,* by M. Sarfatti. ($2.00)
2. *Civil-Military Relations in Argentina, Chile, and Peru,* by Liisa North. ($1.75)
3. *Notes on the Process of Industrialization in Argentina, Chile, and Peru,* by Alcira Leiserson. ($1.75)
4. *Chilean Christian Democracy,* by James Petras. ($1.50)
5. *Social Stratification in Peru,* by M. Larson and A. Bergman. ($3.50)
6. *Modernization and Coercion,* by Mario Barrera. ($1.50)
7. *Latin America: The Hegemonic Crisis and the Military Coup,* by José Nun. ($1.50)
8. *Developmental Processes in Chilean Local Government,* by Peter S. Cleaves. ($1.50)

POPULATION MONOGRAPH SERIES PUBLICATIONS

1. *Return Migration to Puerto Rico,* by José Hernández Alvarez. ($2.00)
2. *Fertility Analysis through Extension of Stable Population Concepts,* by J. R. Rele. ($1.50)
3. *New Life Tables for Latin American Populations in the Nineteenth and Twentieth Centuries,* by Eduardo E. Arriaga. ($2.75)
4. *World Urbanization 1950–1970, Volume 1: Basic Data for Cities, Countries, and Regions,* by Kingsley Davis. ($3.00)
5. *The Female Labor Force in the United States: Demographic and Economic Factors,* by Valerie Kincade Oppenheimer. ($2.50)
6. *Mortality Decline and Its Demographic Effects in Latin America,* by Eduardo E. Arriaga. ($3.00)
7. *Older Male Mortality and Cigarette Smoking: A Demographic Analysis,* by Samuel H. Preston. ($2.00)
8. *Western European Censuses, 1960: An English Language Guide,* by Judith Blake and Jerry J. Donovan. ($3.25)
9. *World Urbanization 1950–1970, Volume II: Analysis of Trends, Relationships, and Development,* by Kingsley Davis. ($3.00)
10. *California's Twenty Million: Research Contributions to Population Policy,* edited by Kingsley Davis and Frederick G. Styles. ($4.25)